C000019220

Shameless scrounge.

You probably already know this, but reviews are the lifeblood of new authors like myself.

Reviews are the best way to let me know what I'm doing right, where I need to up my game, and what to write about next.

More importantly, they help other vegan bakers know if the book might be their kind of thing, so I'd really appreciate it if you shared your thoughts by leaving a review.

Let's get baking!

Mike

To Natalie, who puts up with this kind of nerdiness every day

Beating Eggs & Butter by Mike Sweetman
First published in 2020 by Timberhill Bakery Ltd
27 Old Gloucester Street, London, England, WC1N 3AX
www.mikesweetman.co.uk

Copyright text © 2020 Mike Sweetman
Copyright photographs © 2020 Mike Sweetman
Design and page layout Mike Sweetman
mike@mikesweetman.co.uk

All rights reserved. No part of this publication may be reproduced, transmitted, or stored in a retrieval system, in any form or by an means, without permission in writing from the copyright owner.

Neither the author nor the publisher is responsible for your specific health or allergy needs that may require medical supervision. The author and publisher expressly disclaim responsibility for any adverse effects that may result from the use or application of the recipes and information in this book. Neither the publisher nor the author is engaged in rendering professional advice or services to the individual reader. The ideas, procedures, and suggestions contained in this book are not intended as a substitute for consulting with your physician. Neither the author nor the publisher shall by liable or responsible for any loss or damage allegedly arising from any information or suggestion in this book.

A catalogue record for this book is available from the British Library.

ISBN: 978-1-8383048-0-5

Acknowledgements

Firstly, a big thank you for buying this book - I hope you have as much fun baking with it as I did writing it! A huge thank you to everyone who has supported Natalie and I over the last thirteen years. From the wholefoods stores, restaurant chefs and deli owners when we were based in Wales, to the thousands who rammed Timberhill Bakery in Norwich every week more recently. Some very nice people gave up their time and helped with the bills during the writing of this book: Pippa Craske, Simon Watkins, Imelda Cracknell, Rob Reti, Angela Sawyer of Food Centre Wales, and Chris Holister of Shipton Mill. A couple of personal thank yous from the past: Kevin Field for lighting the baking spark, and the three guys who taught me how to think: Andrew Mendoza, Neil Parker and Fred Pelard. Finally, a special thank you to Joan Stringer who always believed in us, and could sell more of our pies to friends & neighbours than you could think possible.

Contents

HI,
I'M MIKE
AND I'M A
VEGAN BAKER

Back in 2016 I'd just become a vegan, but in my day job as a baker, I was still using a ton of eggs and butter every day. It just didn't feel right.

I wanted to do something about it, but all the vegan baking recipes I found weren't quite good enough for my (mostly non-vegan) customers. I had to find a way of baking without eggs and butter that was so delicious, none of my customers would notice (or care).

When I started looking into it, I was really surprised how many different ways vegan bakers were using to 'beat eggs & butter'. Every baker seemed to have their own favourite method, but no-one was comparing the methods and explaining why they were using chia seeds, or aquafaba, or egg replacers. I started wondering - do all these methods work, and if so, which is the best?

As soon as I started testing, I realised that all these methods were able to make something that was pretty good (and certainly something Instagrammable). But I needed a way of vegan baking that was outright delicious, not just 'delicious *for vegan*'.

Five hundred test bakes later, I concluded that there wasn't a single method to replace eggs & butter in baking; what worked best for cookies didn't necessarily work best for cakes or brownies, and the 'Vegan Baking Wheel' began to take shape.

By choosing the method that best suited whatever I was baking, I was able to create recipes that were just as delicious as their eggs-and-butter equivalents. Soon after, I took the leap and quietly converted my whole bakery counter to plant-based, and waited to see what would happen. I needn't have worried. The only customers who noticed something had changed said the cakes, muffins & brownies had actually improved. Soon, I was baking more than ever.

The first part of this book explains the different techniques and methods that make up the Vegan Baking Wheel. The second section puts this learning to use in 30 super-delicious recipes that have all been developed for home bakers. So get ready to wow your friends and family and show them that baking something truly indulgent just doesn't need eggs or butter!

What to expect from this book

All recipes are tackle-able by newbies

None of these recipes require well-honed baking skills. It may look like some of them have lots of steps, but that's because each recipe is broken down clearly, and none of the steps are complicated.

Easily available and affordable ingredients

90% of the ingredients are available from a supermarke and the other 10% are available from high street whole-foods stores or online.

Same 'base' ingredients used for many of the recipes

Nothing's more expensive than an ingredient you use once, push to the back of the cupboard before realising it's out of date and have to throw it away, so the recipes in each section in this book use very similar 'base' ingredients (flours, sugars and fats).

This doesn't mean the recipes all taste the same; it just means you'll get full use out of the base ingredients you've already bought.

I sometimes break my own rule, and use different base ingredients when a particular flour, sugar or fat gives a **big** difference to flavour or texture, and is **really** worth using.

Just 6 portions per recipe

I've never understood why a lot of recipe books use batch sizes that make 10, 12 or even 20 portions. Great if you have lots of get-togethers, but not so great if you're single, a couple, or just don't have much freezer space.

My recipes are based on a batch size of 6 portions which means you won't get bored of eating the same thing every day or you won't need a ton of freezer space every time you bake.

You won't need fancy kit

Most recipes in this book can be made without a stand mixer or fancy food processor. You'll still need a few pieces of kit, but these are cheap to buy and you may use some of them for general cooking anyway. There's literally no excuse not to get started.

But before we dive in, here's a little about my personal baking journey.

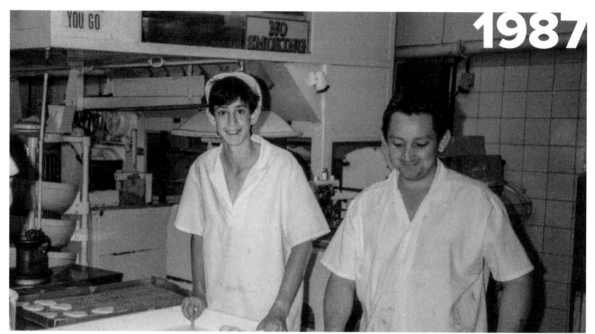

1987

My first taste of baking was a Saturday job in a local bakery in South Wales aged 15, where I made everything from bread, cakes, pies, and doughnuts, and I loved every minute of it. I starting working there during every school and university holidays, before starting a 'proper' career in London.

2007

A hundred years later, I realised I wasn't what the corporate world wanted and decided to get back to baking. My partner Natalie was a vegan, and she had changed my outlook towards food. We combined my love of baking with Natalie's ethical approach to life, and opened Tortoise Bakery ('you can't rush real bread'), an organic sourdough bakery in South Wales, just as the recession was about to hit. Great timing.

After a bumpy few years, the organic market recovered and we started developing a following for our sourdough. By 2012, Tortoise Bakery was a regular on the food festival scene, multiple True Taste Award winners, and suppliers to 100 whole-foods stores across the UK, including Whole Foods Market and Planet Organic. In 2012, we started making vegan brownies as a little side project for ourselves, and when we offered them to our customers, the early-adopting shops started selling them, but only in small numbers. It was still early days for vegan food.

A few years later, interest in vegan food was starting to take off and we began dreaming about a bakery-cafe where vegan food wasn't just an afterthought. We toured the UK visiting our whole-foods customers for inspiration, and after a visit to Arjuna Whole-foods in Cambridge, we popped over to Rainbow Whole-foods in Norwich and were wowed by the city. Its characterful streets and lanes were bristling with independent artisan producers, and this hidden gem is the vegan capital of the UK according to some. We decided to go for it and relocate to the other side of the country to a historic street in the city centre and open what became Timberhill Bakery.

After a slightly shaky start, the gamble started to pay off, and our natural approach to baking began bringing in the love. Plant-based options had equal billing in everything we made and we soon became a destination for vegans. Interestingly, we began to notice that a lot of our plant-based creations were being chosen by real food lovers who weren't necessarily vegan, they just wanted healthy, delicious food. We became very busy, almost every day.

We briefly hit #1 in the city on Trip Advisor, and settled into a regular top-10 spot. It was now time for the next challenge; ditching the eggs and butter in everything we baked. Most of our customers weren't vegan, so we had to make sure everything we baked that was plant-based was so delicious no-one could tell (or would care) that it was vegan. I began the experiments that formed the starting point for this book, and by offering a small range, and picking off the easiest categories to veganize, we were soon able to offer a 100% plant-based bakery counter.

Soon, the bakery was so busy that, despite our short opening hours, 1200 people a week were going out of their way to visit an off-pitch part of Norwich and join the 'happens to be vegan' crowd. Our young team pulled out all the stops every week, buzzing off gallons of espresso and pumping out-of-hours drum and bass. (One reviewer, passing very early one morning, remarked on the energetic vibe prior to opening. That's what having a sub-woofer under the counter does for productivity).

The problem? Development on new vegan treats had basically ground to a halt. We were totally focussed on managing what had become a bit of a beast. Rather than developing new recipes I had become more of a manager than a baker, and while that's what success looks like to lots of people, it just didn't feel like it to me.

So when we were offered the chance to sell the bakery in 2020, I realised this would finally give me the chance to build on what I'd already learned and experiment in new areas of vegan baking. The ultimate goal was to pull the whole thing together into a killer plant-based baking book. Natalie, now used to leaps into the unknown, once again backed me up, and we went for it.

Getting started: ingredients, tips & kit

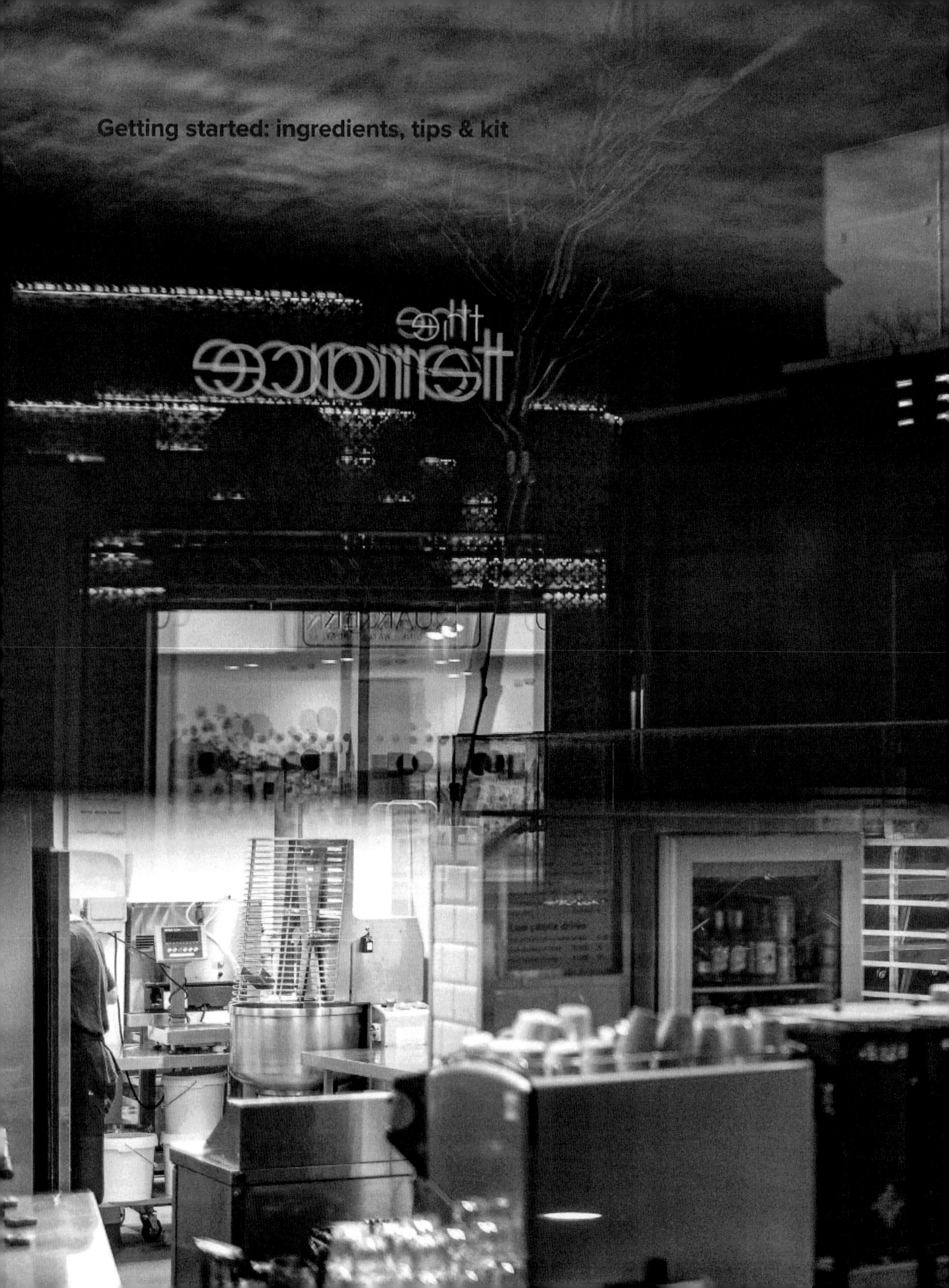

GETTING STARTED:

INGREDIENTS, TIPS & KIT

If you've never baked before

Here are some first principles I wish I'd known when I started baking.

Cake making isn't like cooking

In most types of cooking you can taste and tweak certain things as you go. Add a little seasoning here and there, or reduce a sauce for a little longer to thicken it.

But baking is a one-shot game. You make a cake, put it in the oven, and cross your fingers. You can't tell if a cake batter needs more baking powder as you're mixing it (and no, you can't stop a bake half way through and add it either).

Some very experienced bakers can tell if a batter 'looks wrong' during mixing, but even this gut-feel isn't foolproof. Different cakes need different batter consistencies, so what might look and feel wrong at the mixing stage, might transform into something truly wonderful when it emerges from the oven.

Also, and this is a biggie, when cooking from a recipe you can often swap ingredients you don't like (or don't have) for something you do like (or do have) without having a disaster on your hands.

This is because most ingredients in cooking affect the **flavour** of whatever you're cooking, but in baking, (and especially in cake making), most ingredients affect the **structure** of what you're baking. That's why substitutions are the cause of so many baking fails.

But let's be real - I know that whatever I say, most of you are going to freestyle things and substitute some things anyway, so I cover this later in the book when I explain what you should do, when you're doing what I say you shouldn't really be doing.

Cake making isn't really like bread-making either

And if you're already a great bread baker, you'll know that being a bread legend is less about following a recipe to the last letter, and more about developing a Jedi-like ability to know when a loaf is telling you it wants to be baked. A good bread baker can tweak the 'recipe' of a loaf every day, using their experience to adjust to how the dough is behaving at each stage of the process.

Nailing cakes is easier, or more boring, depending on your outlook to life. As a rebel who loves to bend a rule I hate to say this, but the best way to start is to accurately follow a recipe, (at least to begin with anyway).

Yes, it will seem alien to all veteran bakers who can't resist tweaking a recipe because it 'looks like it needs more flour', but any 'gut-feel' developed from making cakes with eggs and butter needs to take a bit of a back seat here.

Get to know the main baking ingredients

Flour

The biggest ingredient in most recipes, and often the most over-looked. The key to getting to grips with flour is understanding its level of gluten, the natural, magical stretchy protein that helps a batter or dough expand in the oven. In general, the higher the protein content of a flour, the greater the gluten, so using flour with the right protein level is very important in baking.

Commercial bakers have it easier than home bakers. Millers such as Shipton Mill who supply artisan bakeries offer more than a dozen different protein grades, **just within white flour,** and each are designed for a specific purpose.

This is why artisan bakeries don't use all purpose flour; they use cake flour (8-10% protein) for cakes and shortcrust, bread flour (11-13% protein) for bread, and very strong flour (12-15% protein) for croissants and wet doughs like ciabatta or sourdough.

My go-to flour for vegan baking

Overall, my recipes work best with my favourite flour which is white spelt, but all-purpose (or 'AP') is similar enough to be substitutable, just with a few differences.

Why I love using white spelt for vegan cakes

Spelt gives a more strongly bound cake than all-purpose, with a slightly firmer, but still tender crumb. However it has a softer gluten structure, so spelt makes a cake batter that is more elastic and resists cracking better than all-purpose, both very useful properties when baking without eggs. On the downside, using it runs a higher risk of a cake collapsing if the recipe or process isn't followed correctly. I use Shipton Mill's Organic White Spelt; this is roller-milled which makes lighter cakes than stone-ground spelt, due to its lower bran level (it's a 'whiter' type of white flour).

Yes, you can use all-purpose instead of spelt, for an almost-as-good result

When I tested using a mainstream brand of all-purpose instead of spelt I got a fluffier, lighter crumb which was more tender and less likely to sink after baking. However, it was more likely to crack on the surface, had a less indulgent mouthfeel, and had a much stronger 'wheaty' taste making for a less sweet cake than spelt did. However, it was also half the price of spelt, so the choice is yours.

What bakers mean by 'developing gluten'

Now we're going to get a little nerdy. Things don't stop with the protein level of flour; the protein level indicates a flour's *potential* level of gluten. The gluten that's *actually* realised or 'developed' is determined by the baker. In simple terms, this happens in three main ways: how wet a batter or dough is, how well it's mixed, and the fat level used when mixing it.

Very well developed gluten in a sourdough bread dough

More mixing >> means more gluten >> stronger structure >> less tender crumb

When you mix flour with water or plant milk, you are more than just 'mixing together' the flour and liquid evenly. The amount of mixing, kneading, or beating a batter or dough is what determines how much of the flour's **potential** gluten is **actually** developed.

A certain amount of gluten development is needed in cake-making to help give a cake its structure and support its rise. *Trade off alert* - the more you mix a cake, the more gluten is developed and the more bread-like your cake will become. You'll get more rise in the oven ('oven spring'), but also a tougher, more chewy crumb; (great for sourdough bread - definitely not great for a deliciously tender cupcake).

Just because some mixing is good, doesn't mean more is better

The key to a perfectly mixed cake? Striking the balance between just-enough mixing to give the cake some structure, but not too much to give a 'bready' or overly 'springy' texture. The gap between under-mixed and over-mixed is much smaller in cakes and biscuits than it is in bread. Even 10-15 seconds either way can really change the outcome. As it's not easy to judge this sweet spot (especially for beginners), all the recipes in this book have guideline mixing times.

Finally on flour, I've developed some awesome gluten-free recipes where the gluten-free flours really suit the recipe so everyone can bake them and enjoy them.

Fats

More fat >> means less gluten >> weaker structure >> more tender crumb

Fat is your best friend in avoiding a tough, chewy cake as it interrupts the flour from coming into contact with the water or plant milk, so it prevents the process of gluten being developed.

When you add the fat really matters

The best way that fat can stop gluten development is when it makes contact with flour **before** any water or plant milk does. This is why cookies, biscuits and shortcrust pastry, involve 'crumbing' fat with flour well **before** any liquid is added.

The fat coats the flour, minimising its ability to access the liquid and start developing gluten. This 'crumbing' process creates what bakers call a 'short' texture, (which is where shortbread biscuits and shortcrust pastry get their names from).

The opposite is true when making bread, where you need a strongly developed gluten structure, so water is mixed with flour well before any fat is added. In the case of a 'springy' ciabatta loaf, although olive oil is used, it is added at the **end** of the mixing process, and just softens the crumb rather than weakening it.

As cakes fill the gap between 'springy' bread and 'short' scones/ biscuits, my cake recipes add the fat to the flour at the **same time** as the liquid. This still allows a cake's texture to be fine-tuned by altering the amount of fat and plant milk used.

Why I use Sunflower Oil for my cake recipes

I've kept the use of expensive fats like fresh avocados and coconut oil to a minimum, except for recipes where it makes a big difference to flavour, and the cost (or faff) is worth it. For most of my cake recipes, I use a liquid fat like sunflower oil/ canola oil.

Real world factor #1 - using oil is much cheaper than using one of the new plant-based 'baking butters' appearing on the shelves. Baking butters allow a traditional 'creaming' method better than a traditional margarine would, but when I tested cakes made with 'baking butter' I was surprised to find no real flavour benefit over those made with oil.

Real world factor #2 - oil-based recipes are also much easier to make without a stand mixer. Newbies are unlikely to own a stand mixer, and oil-based recipes are **much** easier to mix with an electric hand mixer than 'creamed' baking butter recipes are.

Why I use Vegan Baking Butter for my Cookie recipes

Things are different for cookies. The results are so much better using baking butter rather than oil. The "crumbing" method is critical to nailing the texture of cookies, so I use a baking butter to get that biscuity texture in all my cookie recipes.

Sugars

Sugar brings a lot more than sweetness

Like fat, sugar also plays a part in how gluten develops. In granulated form, sugar attracts water, so it steals some of the plant milk away from the flour, limiting gluten development, making a softer, more tender structure.

Sugar also helps a cake rise. The liquid absorbed by the sugar boils during baking, turning to steam, helping to lift the cake and lighten its texture. (Freestylers reading this - if you reduce the sugar from the level in the recipe it won't just make a less sweet version of the same cake - it will also be chewier, less tender and more dense).

When you add sugar makes a difference

In lots of my recipes I dissolve the sugar with the wet ingredients rather than adding it in with the dry ingredients as in other recipes. This thins out a cake batter and helps replace a little of the extensibility provided by eggs in a traditional recipe.

Dissolving the sugar is easy with a stand mixer, but I appreciate that standing there with a hand mixer for 3 minutes+ is a test of patience, but if you want a smooth top cake with fewer or no cracks, looking good doesn't come easy.

Why you can't swap granulated sugar for a syrup, and expect the same results

Liquid sugars are generally less sweet than granulated sugars, gram for gram. Maple syrup can be 65-85% sugar compared to 100% sugar for brown caster sugar. The difference is mainly water, and this is why substituting sugar for a syrup with no other changes will make a much wetter batter, and make a small, dense and gummy cake that struggles to rise. This doesn't mean you can't bake cakes with syrup - you just need to design the recipe from the outset based on the kind of sugar/syrup you plan to use.

The sugars I prefer to use

Most of my recipes use readily available (and affordable) brown or white caster sugar, which I've found give better results than syrups. For a less processed, alternative sugar, my favourite is coconut sugar which is delicious (but so it should be, given the price). It has a drying effect on a cake, so where I've used it, I've fine-tuned the recipe to compensate. Oh yes, you'll sometimes see me use a mix of light and dark sugars which can help ace the right flavour, colour & texture.

Raising agents

There are two main ways of making a cake rise

The first is the classic and is called 'creaming'. By beating sugar and solid fat together tiny air bubbles are trapped in the batter which expand and rise during baking.

The second method is to use raising agents which come in two forms; baking powder, and bicarbonate of soda (confusingly called baking soda in the US).

Raising agents are not substitutable for each other

Bicarbonate of soda reacts when mixed with an acidic ingredient like apple cider vinegar, causing a fizzing bubbling reaction. When these bubbles are trapped in a cake batter they expand and rise during baking.

Baking powder is a combination of bicarbonate of soda **and** acid, so gram for gram, it contains much less rising power than bicarbonate of soda. (Freestylers - this means you can't substitute one for the other and expect the same raising effect).

I use the more powerful bicarbonate of soda in recipes with lots of added fruit, vegetables or nuts (the "additions"). These kind of batters need the fire-power of bicarbonate of soda to help a heavier cake rise.

Bicarbonate of soda generally gives a less uniform, more open crumb structure with a mixture of larger and smaller air pockets. It has to be used very sparingly because lots of larger air pockets increases the risk of either a cake collapsing, or it having a very crumbly texture.

Another important difference between the raising agents is the speed at which they work. Bicarbonate of soda works extremely quickly, helping to raise a cake in the early part of the bake, whereas baking powder generally works more slowly. Recipes can use a combination of both types of raising agents, to evenly raise the sides of a cake (which rise earlier in a bake) and the centre of a cake (which rises later in a bake).

Both agents have a slightly salty, bitter, metallic taste which is hard to detect at low levels but can be pretty disgusting at high levels. Everyone has a different sensitivity to this, so I've kept the levels low in my recipes.

Why I use apple cider vinegar in lots of my recipes

Even though baking powder already contains acid, I still add a little vinegar or acidic juice to most of my recipes as it releases a little extra lift and can neutralise the bitter taste of baking powder. Extra acid has to be used carefully though, or you can either get an over-reaction from the raising agents (and a fast-rising cake that can collapse), or a slightly sour, vinegary taste in the finished cake. I've found apple cider vinegar to be the most subtle way to add extra acid.

Get used to the gram scales (see Kit section)

As raising agents and acids need to be used sparingly, lots of recipes in this book use measurements as light as a couple of grams. Trust me on this; accurately weighing these ingredients in particular will make a **big** difference to your baking.

Why baking your cake soon after mixing is important

To raise a cake properly, three things need to happen in the right order, and at the right time.

> 1. '**Fizzing**': raising agents are activated during the mixing process creating lots of little bubbles, which are trapped in the batter.

> **2. Rising**: the batter is heated in the oven, forcing the trapped air bubbles to expand and lift, making the cake rise.

> **3. Setting:** the batter starts to set, supporting the risen cake.

For recipes that only use bicarbonate of soda, all the fizzing starts as soon as mixing begins. So if a fully mixed cake batter is left to stand while the oven is warming up, some of those precious bubbles will rise to the surface and escape, reducing the lifting effect of the raising agents.

Recipes using baking powder are generally more forgiving to baking straight after mixing, especially if they use 'slow-acting' baking powders which are engineered to release only 30-40% of their 'fizzing' action during mixing, and another 60-70% during baking. However, that's still 30-40% which is happening during and straight after mixing, so the same rule still applies; bake your cake as soon as possible after mixing.

Oven tips

Why baking at the right temperature matters so much

Oven temperature affects the speed at which a batter sets, so a cake baked in an oven that's too cool will set too late to prevent those air bubbles from escaping through a surface that's still in a semi-liquid form.

And, without the air bubbles giving the batter its volume, the cake shrinks back and sinks. This usually happens in the centre of a cake, because the centre gets less heat than the outside of a cake so is most at risk of not setting early enough to trap in the air bubbles.

In contrast, an oven that's too hot can cause setting to start too early. The surface of the cake sets before the rest of the batter has finished rising. This leads to an under-risen, small or really domed cake, with cracks on the top, as the batter is still trying to rise and crack its way through a surface that has already set.

Why pre-heating your oven matters

In general, it takes much longer to heat a domestic oven properly than it takes to weigh and mix a cake batter. So whilst it's a good idea to start weighing or preparing ingredients whilst your oven is warming up, you should only start mixing once your oven is fully up to temperature.

Every oven is different

You've probably heard this a hundred times, but it's worth repeating. Baking needs **your** feel and knowledge of **your** oven to get the best out of it.

The baking times and temperatures in this book are guidelines and should be viewed as **starting points** for the first time you bake a recipe. All my recipes were developed with a fairly new, small oven that I thought would be close to a typical home kitchen.

But just for fun, I tested the same programme on a much older, seen-better-days home oven. Firstly, my trusty oven thermometer showed that I needed to crank the dial to $200^{\circ}C$ to get the **actual** temperature inside the oven to be $155^{\circ}C$. But even then, it still wasn't baking through to the centre, leaving a gummy crumb, (I suspected a slower fan speed was the cause). It ended up needing a real $200^{\circ}C$ to bake properly, and a reduced baking time of about a third or it burned on the outside. Bottom line? You may need to tweak the baking times and temperatures a little.

Other tips

Ditch the cups

You've probably also read this many times, so I'll keep this one brief. Digital scales are so cheap nowadays and so accurate that the single biggest thing you can do to raise your baking game is to switch to using weights rather than volumes.

I see the appeal of weighing by volumes - it can be quicker, it seems more straightforward and more hands-on, but for reliable results, accuracy is king.

Mixing times and speed matter

You'll notice that lots of my recipes have specific times and speeds for mixing. When testing the mixing times for this book I bought a cheap hand mixer and a domestic stand mixer to fine tune my mixing times.

Once I'd adjusted the mixing times from my commercial kit, the times needed for domestic kit were very similar for both hand mixers and stand mixers. Whilst all mixers are different, as a general guide Speed 1 equates to slow, Speed 2 or 3 to medium, and Speeds 4 or 5 to fast.

Cool before tipping out & cutting

The cake is still finishing off baking whilst cooling. Tipping out and cutting it before it fully cools means it won't be fully baked and may turn it into a crumbly mess. Allow an hour to cool before tipping out.

Don't let your hard work go to waste; storage

Once a cake, cookie or brownie has cooled, show it some love by storing it in an air tight container to help keep it moist and fresh. You can extend the shelf life by refrigerating it, but bring it out of the fridge two hours before serving.

If you want to freeze any cakes, freeze them on the day of baking in an airtight container, and store them for around a month. They will begin to dry out after that. It can also be handy to cut or portion your cake before freezing, so you can defrost a slice at a time.

Lo-Fi Kit

Why you don't need the best kit

While having the best tools for any job or craft always helps, the good news is for cake making, the best tools only makes a small difference.

Lo-Fi Kit

Electric hand mixer
While it's possible to mix a batter by hand, given the cost of electric hand mixers nowadays, buying one is a bit of a no-brainer.

Alongside my pro mixer and stand mixer, I bought a £10 hand mixer to test my recipes with, and I achieved almost identical results with the £10 hand mixer as with the £300 stand mixer.

More importantly, I didn't need to change the process in any way; I could use the same mixing times for both the hand and stand mixer and get very similar results.

Gram scales (digital)
These are also so cheap nowadays, (mine were £10) and so accurate, they're also a great buy. Mine measure two decimal places, which might sound like overkill, but when you are weighing a couple of grams of salt or baking powder, the more accurate you can be the better. Nerdy heaven.

Oven thermometer
Another low-cost investment with a high bang-for-buck. Oven temperature is very important when baking, and your oven dial is almost certainly lying to you; using an oven thermometer will be a big help.

Timer
After weighing correctly and baking at the right temperature, the next most important factor when baking cakes is mixing for the correct length of time. I've put some guideline mixing times into every recipe and using a timer is the best way to follow the recipe closely. Like eveything else in the Lo-Fi Kit list, they are very affordable so every baker should have one.

Tins

Brownie

Loaf

Round

Mini Loaf

PME®

Muffin

If you haven't bought tins yet . . .

. . . then try to buy tins with dimensions as close as possible to the ones I've used. The dimensions matter much more than the brand of tin. Most recipes in this book were developed with the five most commonly used tins:

Round   **L 20 x W 20cm (8 x 8in)**   **H 5cm (2in)**
I'm using one made by PME and you'll need to add on a baking belt if you want super-flat layer cakes. You'll need a removable base one if you want to also use the tin to make my Peppermint Cheesecake recipe.

Mini Loaf   **L 8.5 x W 5.5cm (3.25 x 2.25 in)   H 3.5cm (1.5 in)**
Again, mine's by PME with space for 8 mini loaves. The lengths and widths are measured half way up the mini loaf, so when comparing tins, the measurements are larger at the top and slightly smaller at the base.

Brownie   **L 22 x W 22cm (9 x 9in)**   **H 5cm (2in)**
I'm using one by Alan Silverwood with a removable base

1lb Loaf   **L 16cm x W 10cm (6.5in x4in)   H 7.5cm (3in)**
Again, I'm using Alan Silverwood's. "One Pound" loaf tins vary a lot in capacity and shape; this one is at the bigger end of the spectrum

Muffin Tin/ Cupcake
I'm using one from Delia Smith's range, again by Alan Silverwood

Can I use (similar) tins I've already got?
Of course - you might not get that last 5% of perfection, but what you bake will still be great. If the tin I suggest is a size halfway between two tins you already own, use the larger of your tins to make sure the batter doesn't overspill the tin.

When I develop a recipe, I decide the ingredients, baking instructions and tin all at the same time. Each of these interact with each other, so if you change one of them you need to tweak the others to compensate.

But back in the real world of home baking, no-one wants to buy a new tin to match one in a recipe book, so don't let this put you off. Even if you bake a cake or brownie that isn't perfect it'll still have been made by you, and will still be more delicious than anything you can buy at the supermarket.

You can worry about more tins later - the main thing is to start with what you've got.

Wish List

Nice to haves

Stand mixer

Better than a hand mixer for two reasons: the first of which is consistency. It's easier to over-mix with a hand mixer than a stand mixer because the amount you move your hand around the bowl affects the amount the batter mixes.

The second benefit is speed and convenience. You can walk away from a stand mixer, whilst it's mixing, so you can start weighing out the next stage or get your tins prepared whilst the mixing is happening. If you're baking regularly for bake sales or farmer's markets, get one and you won't look back.

Food processor

Helpful for: grating things like carrots and courgettes, dicing nuts into smaller pieces, and for making icing (see Iced Lemon Loaf Cake recipe).
Essential for: making cashew cream frosting or cashew cheesecake.

Coffee grinder / spice grinder

Useful if you want more fragrant spices by grinding them yourself; for example, cardamom seeds are incredibly more aromatic and powerful when freshly ground.

Remember to trim back the weights of freshly ground spices by around 20% or so, and you'll get all the extra flavour without them overpowering everything else.

For the Christmas list

Stick blender	- if you plan to make ganache and want it super-smooth
Cake lifter	- if you plan to make layer cakes
Turntable	- for frosting/ decorating
Piping nozzles and bags	- for cupcakes
Probe thermometer	- to test core temperatures
Portioner (ice-cream scoop)	- to speed up scaling muffins
Cooling racks	- to speed up cooling
Squeezy bottle & nozzle	- for applying thin icings in a decorative way
Juicer and micro planer	- for juicing and zesting

How to replace eggs & butter in baking

My tests filled this table 4 times over

HOW TO REPLACE EGGS & BUTTER IN BAKING

Starting with cakes

When I started researching plant-based baking, I was quickly overwhelmed and very confused. Bakers couldn't seem to agree on what the best way of making vegan cakes was, let alone how to make vegan cookies, brownies and cupcakes.

I decided to find out for myself and pick off the cake challenge first.

What would success look (taste) like?

A method that works for a host of recipes
In my tests I excluded cake-making methods that used an ingredient with a distinctive flavour, like banana or apple sauce. I knew these methods definitely worked in certain types of cakes, but I wasn't looking for a series of stand-alone recipes, I wanted a method that worked across a wide range of cakes, that could take some customisation depending on how it was being used.

Flavour
I was looking for the closest possible flavour to the richness of butter without a distinctive flavour that might clash with the main flavour of a cake.

Texture
A "short", tender, cake-like crumb was very important. Not chewy and bread-y on the one hand, and not crumbly and fragile on the other.

Mouth-feel
The perfect level of moistness would be critical. Not too dry and definitely not too "claggy" (where it starts to form a ball in your mouth), no thank you.

Practicality
As a commercial baker this one is a biggie for me. Nothing too faffy or inconsistent. It's gotta just work. Must be affordable to make too.

From my initial research I narrowed down the options into 5 methods that, on paper, looked the most likely to succeed.

Using constant sugar and fat levels, I made the same simple vanilla cake with each method, and to make the test as fair as possible, I tweaked each method dozens and dozens of times to get the best out of it.

Finally, I took the best recipe from each method and compared them with each other and here are the results:

Which method makes the best vegan cake?

1. Creaming: the old-school method

If you bought a vegan cake back in the year 2000 it would have probably been made using this method. It's the closest thing to a traditional eggs-and-butter cake and involves creaming sugar with a margarine or plant-butter. This creamed mixture is then combined with a vegan 'egg' made with an egg replacer product, (like Ener-G or Orgran), and then flour and plant milk are added in three, alternating, stages.

Tasting cakes made with the Creamed method

This method gave good flavour and a lovely cake-like texture. A smidge on the dry side for some, but nothing a little frosting or icing wouldn't take care of. The main drawback was the faffy process, which meant achieving consistent results would be much harder for newbies. I was also concerned that using 'composite ingredients' like margarine and egg replacer wouldn't suit the whole-foods crew.

2. Chia: the whole-foods method

By the time I'd set up my bakery in 2007, the chia method had taken over from the creaming method as the main way to make vegan cakes. Most vegans at the time were heavily into the whole-foods/ organic food scene and the chia method substituted egg replacers with chia seeds, (a positive ingredient with well-known health benefits), and replaced margarine with a whole oil such as sunflower oil.

Tasting cakes made with the Chia method

This method gave pretty good results, **for vegan cake**, but it wouldn't convince anyone that vegan baking can beat traditional baking. On the plus side, this cake was less crumbly than the creamed cake, but it was heavier and more dense, and had a slight savoury flavour that seemed to mask the sugar & vanilla. Switching to white chia seeds or flax seeds made little difference, and the cakes made with this method weren't as pretty or smooth-surfaced as ones made with the other methods. Overall, just pretty good.

#3. Aquafaba: the hyped method

Most of you reading this will probably already know that aquafaba is the liquid in a can or carton of chickpeas. You also probably know that when you whisk it for a *very* long time, it whips up to a fluffy light foam in an amazingly similar way to egg whites.

Essentially, aquafaba is an egg **white** replacer (not a **whole egg** replacer) so perhaps using it to make cakes is a little unfair. But lots of recipes claim big things for it, so it earned its place in this test. Many recipes using aquafaba make the foam first and then fold it gently into the batter. Some recipes add sugar to this foam, and whisk it again (as if making meringue) and *then* fold it in. Others just whisk aquafaba in a jug,

by hand, for say 30 seconds, and add it to the wet mix. After testing all three methods (many times), with different whisking speeds and different mixing times, none of the foaming methods gave a better result than the simple hand-whisk method, so I used the hand whisk version to represent aquafaba in this comparison.

Tasting cakes made with the Aquafaba method

Cakes made using this method were great looking with the second biggest volume of all the methods. They were also the most moist, with a sticky, wet crumb, giving a touch less crumbliness and an excellent shelf life. This might suit a cafe making highly decorated cakes, usually eaten with a fork, where shelf life is as much of a concern as flavour & texture.

The bad news? The texture was right on the edge of being claggy and a little hard to eat, so this method would probably struggle to make a cake with any moist additions, like a carrot cake. After trying sixteen variations with drier batters, I found it was *possible* to solve the stickiness problem but this created new problems; either less rise or a less enjoyable mouth-feel.

More importantly, whilst taste is subjective, for me at least, the flavour didn't hit the spot as the aquafaba seemed to dilute the sweetness significantly. My conclusion was that aquafaba could help solve a crumbliness problem as part of a recipe, but as a method in itself, it failed to live up to the hype. I came away from this one slightly disappointed.

4 'Just Oil': the laziest method

This method has been on the rise in the last couple of years. There is no specific ingredient trying to replace eggs in these kind of recipes, they just use a liquid fat such as sunflower oil. I can see the appeal of this type of recipe; they have the fewest ingredients (so are the cheapest) and have the simplest method. They rely on liquid fat being combined with flour, plant milk and sugar, to develop a more extensible batter than one made with a solid fat. I love a simple solution, so this one had to be included in the test.

Tasting cakes made with 'just oil'

The good news first: this method won the rise test with great volume. It made a good looking cake with a lovely surface finish. On the downside, the colour was pale rather than golden, it had a bready texture, and a bland flavour that lacked richness. More of an issue was the oil didn't 'emulsify' (or fully combine) well with the rest of the batter, so it left a slight taste of fried fat, a little like a doughnut, (but not in a good way). Overall, if you want something that looks good for your Instagram, this gives simple, low cost, and great looking results. But if you're into flavour and texture, this method just doesn't cut it.

5. Plant Protein: the new method

Aside from providing some flavour and colour, eggs have three main roles in cake-making: combining the batter ('emulsify'), helping the batter to rise ('leaven'), and helping the batter set ('coagulate') in the oven.

I knew from the "just oil' test that a batter made with liquid oil could partly achieve all three of these; it could be (partly) emulsified, extensible enough to be risen just with raising agents and, was able to set fully. What was missing was that final emulsification, colour, richness of flavour, and short texture. So the crude thinking behind the Plant Protein method was to build on the 'just oil' method in the hope that by adding a high protein ingredient I could maintain the positives while removing the drawbacks. I tested three types of plant protein to see which might work; hemp, potato and pea. I excluded soya protein because although I suspected it may be effective (I've seen it being used by some larger bakeries), it's quite divisive in the vegan world and it's also an allergen which limits its potential appeal slightly.

Tasting the Plant Protein cakes

Hemp protein has great eco credentials so it's the one I tried first. I really wanted this to work but ended up rejecting it quickly. I could really taste the hemp flavour which didn't work for me at all. It also made everything slightly green, so it was a definite no.

Next up was potato protein, which wasn't available in retail shops at the time of testing but I wanted the test to be future proof. This gave amazing volume, (it was the largest cake of all the trials), and the protein is very concentrated so only a tiny amount was needed to give a fantastic looking cake.

Whilst the potato protein cakes avoided many of the drawbacks of the other methods, (they weren't dry, claggy or fried-fatty tasting), they did have a bready texture and a very bland flavour. So think of potato protein as a very effective egg-white replacer, with lots of potential for plant-based macaron or meringue. Not the winner in this test.

Finally onto pea protein, and I immediately loved this. This method gave less volume than potato protein but had a much richer flavour and a shorter, more tender, cake-like crumb.

Results

The winning cake was the one made with pea protein. The sweetness of the cake wasn't dulled as with chia seed and aquafaba. Nor was it neutral and bland like the cakes made either with 'just oil', or with potato protein. While it was slightly less fluffy than the creamed method cake, it was less claggy and sticky than the aquafaba and 'just oil' cakes. Although the pea protein cake had a slightly shorter shelf life than all but the creamed cake, I felt the extra deliciousness more than compensated.

The pea actually added flavour by seeming to bring together the sugar, fat and vanilla to form a harmonious, deep and indulgent thing of its own. It had a similar effect on richness as adding egg yolk to a traditional cake batter. I was really impressed by the cake made using this method.

What sealed the deal was the mouth-feel; it was just a really enjoyable thing to eat. When adding pea protein to a cake batter, you need to reduce the flour to keep the hydration or 'wetness' of the batter constant. Compared to the other test cakes, I was able to reduce the flour by 13% - 23%. This reduced the gluten level enough to give a short and tender texture, whilst still having a well bound and moist crumb. The cherry on top was that once I'd nailed the best recipe, it was super-simple to make, with super-consistent results.

Flavour
1st   Pea Protein
2nd   Creamed
3rd   Aquafaba
4th   Chia
5th   Just Oil

Texture/ Mouth-feel
=1st   Pea Protein
=1st   Creamed
3rd   Aquafaba
4th   Just Oil
5th   Chia

Shelf Life
=1st   Aquafaba
=1st   Just Oil
3rd   Chia
4th   Pea Protein
5th   Creamed

Practicality
1st   Just Oil
2nd   Pea Protein**
3rd   Aquafaba
4th   Chia
5th   Creamed

*** simple to make, but you do have to buy the Pea Protein*

Cost
1st   Just Oil
2nd   Aquafaba*
=3rd   Chia
=3rd   Creamed
5th   Pea Protein

** if you normally buy chickpeas then Aquafaba is free*

Leader-board

1st   **Pea Protein**
2nd   **Creamed**
3rd   **Aquafaba**
4th   **Just Oil**
5th   **Chia**

What would customers think?

Then came the tough part. My opinion didn't really matter, nor did my partner Natalie's. This wasn't a lab test or some personal obsession. (OK, it became a kind of obsession). What really mattered were the twelve hundred people coming through the doors of Timberhill Bakery every week.

So for a couple of weeks, I made sample versions of our best selling Lemon & Raspberry cake using pea protein and asked customers for their feedback. It was all very positive. But we had very nice customers - maybe they were just being polite? Would they actually buy a plant-based cake if they weren't vegan themselves? There was only one way to find out.

Cake that happens to be vegan

We converted our Lemon cake first and labelled it "Happens to be Vegan". We held our breath and . . . there was no dip in sales. I cleared every table which had a Lemon cake on it I asked customers what they thought. They would say "something is different." When I asked "different how?", they'd say, " different in a good way".

We converted two more cakes. Sales held up. We went for it and converted all our cakes to plant-based recipes. Local press picked it up. The bakery got busier. Cake sales actually went **up**.

What was most interesting was that the bulk of the extra sales were coming from our regular, traditional customers rather than from a huge influx of new vegan customers.

A whole counter of plant-based treats

The next step was to convert everything else on the counter to plant-based recipes, including savoury muffins, scones, brownies, florentines, cookies, cinnamon rolls and croissants.

What interested me at this point was that other products needed different solutions to the one that worked for cakes. By the end of the process I began to suspect that some of the methods I'd rejected for cakes might be perfect for other products.

Beyond cake

When I finally had the time to dig deeper and test my findings fully, I started by trying to understand why certain products suited some methods better than others.

As I continued testing, I compared my results and found that although there wasn't a single method of replacing eggs and butter across all plant-based baking, there was still a pattern.

A breakthrough came when I realised that the bakes that shared the same 'best method' tended to have similar textures, and that these textures could be grouped into 5 different textures:.

'Airy' texture   - super-light, like macarons and meringue

'Short'   - verging on crumbly, like biscuits and scones

'Tender'   - cake-like, in-between Airy and Short

'Springy'   - where gluten has been developed, like buns and croissants

'Strong'   - verging on chewy, tightly bound, like chewy cookies

I mapped these onto a baking 'wheel' and overlaid the methods and products to represent the spectrum of textures that can be achieved.

The Plant-Based 'Baking Wheel'

The wheel doesn't cover every type of baked product, just the main ones that rely on the functional properties of eggs and butter during a baking process.

The purpose of the wheel is to help identify which plant-based methods suit certain products, by linking them back to texture.

It also provides a valuable short-cut to the process of developing new plant-based recipes. By narrowing down the methods that are most likely to work, I could waste less time trying to perfect the wrong kind of recipe, and more time on fine-tuning recipes that used the best method from the outset.

Areas of the Baking Wheel covered in this book

For this book I've chosen recipes from the three segments of the wheel that are the most tackle-able and most likely to be baked at home.

'Tender'

The Tender segment contains most types of cakes that have a melt-in-the-mouth texture, somewhere in between super-light ('Airy') and verging on crumbly ('Short').

THE PLANT-BASED BAKING WHEEL

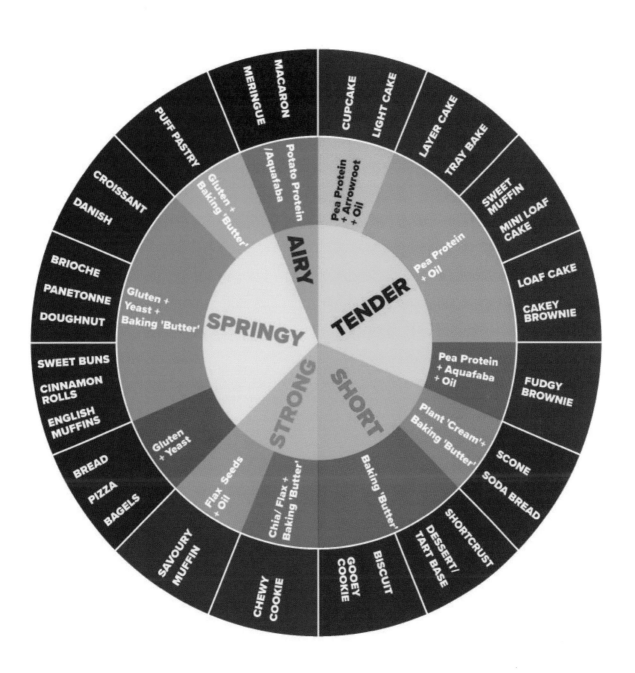

Inner wheel categories: AIRY, TENDER, SPRINGY, STRONG, SHORT

Ingredient segments:
- Potato Protein / Aquafaba
- Gluten + Baking 'Butter'
- Pea Protein + Arrowroot + Oil
- Pea Protein + Oil
- Gluten + Yeast + Baking 'Butter'
- Pea Protein + Aquafaba + Oil
- Gluten + Yeast
- Plant 'Cream' + Baking 'Butter'
- Flax Seeds + Oil
- Chia / Flax + Baking 'Butter'
- Baking 'Butter'

Outer ring bakes:
- MACARON
- MERINGUE
- PUFF PASTRY
- CROISSANT
- DANISH
- BRIOCHE
- PANETONNE
- DOUGHNUT
- SWEET BUNS
- CINNAMON ROLLS
- ENGLISH MUFFINS
- BREAD
- PIZZA
- BAGELS
- SAVOURY MUFFIN
- CHEWY COOKIE
- GOOEY COOKIE
- BISCUIT
- DESSERT/TART BASE
- SHORTCRUST
- SODA BREAD
- SCONE
- FUDGY BROWNIE
- CAKEY BROWNIE
- LOAF CAKE
- MINI LOAF CAKE
- SWEET MUFFIN
- TRAY BAKE
- LAYER CAKE
- LIGHT CAKE
- CUPCAKE

A lot of 'Tender' cake recipes use similar ingredients and methods as their starting point, and their key ingredient is pea protein.

Once you've learned how to bake one of these recipes, you'll be able to turn your hand to the others easily. Their varying degrees of richness, texture and colour are achieved through tweaking ingredients, ratios & methods.

As we move towards either end of the Tender segment, the pea protein method needs a little fine-tuning. Cupcakes sit at the end nearest to Airy, and for these I've reduced the pea and added a little starch (arrowroot). This sacrifices some ultimate flavour to achieve the lightest texture.

Fudgy Brownies sit at the opposite end of the Tender segment nearest to Short, and for these I've added some aquafaba. This is to partially utilise the micro-bubbles that can be created with aquafaba, to give a velvety, smooth texture which perfectly suits a gooey, indulgent brownie.

'Short'

I decided to base these recipes on dedicated plant-based 'baking butter'. The availability of these is rising and they give better results than vegan spreads or margarines which have lower melting points.

'Strong'

The key ingredients in these recipes are chia seeds and flax seeds, and all my recipes use them in their ground form. Mainstream supermarkets are now stocking pre-milled chia or flax, but if you can only get hold of (or prefer to use) whole seeds, you can grind these yourself in a domestic coffee grinder to achieve the same result.

While chia and flax can be substituted with each other, they have their differences. Using chia rather than flax will give a darker, slightly grey crumb, a less savoury flavour, and a tighter binding effect for the same weight used.

Tendered   £10.00
Change   £5.20

Today's
Soup:
Spiced
Root Veg

Organic roast parsnips,
potatoes and carrots blended
with warming winter spices,
fresh ginger and garlic

HOW TO REPLACE GLUTEN, EGGS & BUTTER IN BAKING

Why you can't just sub for a gluten-free flour

Most of the recipes in this book already cater to those with a gluten-sensitivity, as most are based on lower-gluten spelt flour. I found that when I developed a recipe with spelt, I could substitute with plain/ all purpose flour, but it didn't work as well the other way around.

But spelt is not gluten-free. When I substituted spelt for a gluten-free flour, my recipes just didn't work. (The brownie recipes in this book are the exception; you can substitute very well for buckwheat flour).

So hacking gluten-free meant going back to the drawing board. I knew it would be tricky, from the dozens of vegan-gluten-free cakes Natalie and I have tasted over the years, from bakeries in many different countries.

Whilst we've had some memorable vegan cakes, (the most recent was at Txarloska Pastelería in Bilbao), the hit rate for **vegan-and-gluten-free** cakes has always been low, even when we've visited ultra-progressive, super-cool places in California.

When I researched non-vegan gluten-free cakes, they almost always rely on, you guessed it, a ton more eggs than normal. So starting with no eggs meant that swapping the flour and hoping for the best was never really going to work.

Gluten-free needs a different approach

My favourite method for vegan cakes (Pea Protein) didn't work

I started with the most obvious trial, by trying to replicate the additional eggs used in egg-based gluten-free cakes by using more pea protein. I also tested adding the pea protein at different stages of the mixing process.

Neither worked. Pea protein is quite a strong binder; the higher level was inhibiting the rise, giving a dense cake with a cracked surface.

Using chia seeds didn't hit the spot either; the strong binding effect also gave a dense cake (but without the richness of pea).

Next, I tested aquafaba as this gave a weaker binding effect in my vegan cake trials and I did get a slightly less dense result, but now I had a really soggy crumb.

This wasn't a huge surprise as aquafaba gives a wetter, slacker bind than pea protein. I tried tweaking with a drier batter and lower levels of pea and lower oil. None of these really worked. I seemed to solve one problem only to create a new one.

The biggest problem across all the trials so far was that the delicious cakes were always too soggy, and the ones that weren't soggy were far from delicious. Time to switch things up.

Experimenting with starches

Starches are common in gluten-free and vegan cake recipes, but I'm a bit reluctant to use them as I've always found they can give a weird, slightly furry mouth-feel. But the key to hacking is to keep an open mind. I needed something to avoid a soggy bake and, given starches' ability to absorb moisture, I went back to basics, removed the pea protein and started experimenting with starches.

The good news - starches were definitely binding the batter. The bad news - the amount needed to bind also gave that super-dry-cotton-wool-type mouth-feel I was desperate to avoid.

The breakthrough came when I tried pea protein and starch together. Pea protein seems to bind whilst locking moisture into the batter (giving a moist mouth-feel), whereas starch seems to bind whilst sucking moisture out of the batter (giving a dry mouth-feel).

Together, they balanced each other out and gave great binding properties, with a moist texture without the sogginess. Progress at last.

Arrowroot easily won the starch head-to-head

Next, I tested different types of starch and found that grain-based starch (corn flour) gave nowhere near as good results as root/ tuber based starch (tapioca, potato and arrowroot). Overall, my favourite by far was arrowroot for its gentle bind, smooth mouth-feel and neutral flavour.

My favourite gluten-free flour(s)

Single flours vs blends

I knew from other gluten-free recipes that lots of bakers find it essential to use a blend of flours, so in my tests of 9 different flours, I included blends of the flours that individually gave promising results.

The best single flour: Brown Rice Flour

While no single flour gave better results than blends, if I had to develop a gluten-free cake recipe with only one flour, it would be brown rice flour. It's a wholemeal flour (so tastes very slightly like a cake made with brown flour) but if you wanted a wholefoods-type cake, a recipe developed using just brown rice flour would give you something you could enjoy.

Developing a custom blend

Developing a cake with an indulgent feel meant finding the best blend. I started with Doves Farm Plain White (a blend of rice, potato, tapioca, maize and buckwheat). It gave a solid, if not amazing result, and would have made my recipes slightly easier to make, providing you were using that exact same flour.

How to replace gluten, eggs & butter in baking

The problem with ready-made blends is that they are all different. So if I developed recipes using Doves Farm's blend for example, and you use a different blend, you're going to get very different results. Instead I made a blend that anyone can put together themselves, and get great results when used in my recipes.

Winning Blend: white rice flour & ground almonds (almond 'flour')

A 50:50 blend of white rice flour and ground almonds was head and shoulders over anything else I tried. A few tweaks were needed to the other ingredients and method to get the best out of it, but the combination of the very fine and relatively bland white rice flour, and the very coarse and full flavoured ground almonds stole the show.

Other gluten-free hacks learned along the way

#1 - Mix for much longer

Ground almonds can be grainy unless aggressively mixed, but as there's no gluten development to worry about, I ended up increasing the mix times significantly, safe in the knowledge I wasn't creating a tough cake.

#2 - Use a lower oil level

The downside of the longer mix time was the ground almonds started releasing some of their oil into the batter. I ended up almost halving the oil level in most recipes to compensate for this, and still got a lovely rich mouth-feel without the dreaded crumbliness.

#3 - Use sugar with a low molasses content

I love using dark sugars with tons of natural flavour but their extra stickiness doesn't suit gluten-free flours, especially in larger cakes. Drier sugars like coconut sugar or white caster work best in larger cakes and smaller cakes like muffins can take a blend of white and brown/ demerara. Syrups gave poor results in almost every test I did.

Happens to be gluten-free

Combined, the arrowroot, white rice flour and ground almonds gave delicious flavour and the perfect short texture without the crumbliness. They were so good, I'd happily sell them to a non-gluten-free customer knowing that they **may** notice there was something slightly different, but they'd be enjoying them too much to care.

SUBSTITUTIONS & TROUBLE - SHOOTING

You shouldn't, but you're going to anyway.

You shouldn't substitute any of the ingredients in any of my recipes, but I know you're going to anyway. So if you find yourself asking 'do I **really** need that pea protein?' (answer - yes), here's the unofficial rules as to what you should do, when you're doing what you shouldn't be doing in the first place . . .

Substitutions that generally don't work

If it's a core ingredient in the batter like flour, sugar or fat, then changing these should be avoided as it'll change the recipe's fundamental ratios.

In areas of baking like bread-making you can change the flour, water and salt levels and still get great (but different results). In cake-making, freestyling the ratios is essentially creating a new recipe, so unless you're deliberately trying to create a new recipe (and are expecting a few fails along the way), it's best to focus your creativity in other areas.

Substitutions that *can* work, (if you put some thought into it)

Changing the **type** of core ingredients (flour, sugar, fat) can often work, but only if the substituting ingredient has similar properties (such as moisture levels, binding qualities or how it behaves at temperature).

For example, spelt and all-purpose flour are essentially interchangeable as they have similar properties (weak gluten structure, low-ish moisture absorption). Switching spelt for 'strong bread flour' however, is a much bigger change as the gluten properties are very different.

Likewise sugar; changing from a dry granulated sugar to a liquid syrup is unlikely to work without adjustments elsewhere as the moisture level, sweetness and crumb structure will all be affected by the sugar choice.

Substitutions that usually work, (but still need some thought)

Generally, "Additions" are added after a batter's been mixed so have a much lower impact on the fundamental structure of a cake than the core ingredients like flour or sugar.

So swapping raisins for cranberries or hazelnuts say, will affect the recipe very little, so have fun and experiment, just try to use additions which are similar in size, weight and moisture content.

A recipe optimised for fresh raspberries will assume some moisture release from the fresh fruit compared to a recipe that's been optimised for dried fruit. So rather than swapping for dried raspberries for example, substitute for a different fresh fruit (like kiwis) instead.

Tin size substitution

The obvious one first - the bigger the cake and/ or the deeper the batter in a tin, the lower the temperature and longer the bake time you'll need.

Large cake recipes, baked in smaller tins - a solid bet

One of my big loaf tin recipes will generally work well divided into mini loaf tins or muffins. The shallower batter and smaller shapes mean the main tweak you'll need is a shorter bake time in a slightly hotter oven.

Small cake recipes, baked in a larger tin - less reliable

However, recipes developed as a cupcakes or muffin are generally wetter than those that have been designed from the outset to be loaf cakes. The heat penetrates a small cake so much faster than a deep, large loaf cake that the recipe can use a wetter batter with less risk of collapsing. (And, as wetter batters usually make more moist cakes, a baker is always trying to push a recipe to be as wet as possible whilst avoiding collapsing).

So if you baked a recipe designed for 6 muffins as a single large loaf cake, the heat penetration will be so much slower in the loaf tin that the rise, setting and structure of the cake will be affected and the top could settle back, causing the cake to sink.

While you may still get pretty good results, if you like to tweak things you can offset this in various ways; baking at a lower temperature and for longer than the muffin recipe, trimming the raising agents back by a third or so (to slow down the rise), and trimming back the plant milk a smidge. Embrace your inner nerd and make notes about what you did, how it turned out and be prepared for some trial and error.

Batch size hacks

Increase baking time as you scale up (usually, at the same temperature)

This varies with the equipment being used, but as a rough rule of thumb, bake for 10% longer when doubling the amount of cake being baked. That's for a good oven, (so in my dodgy home oven I'd probably bake 15-20% longer).

As the batch size increases, it's extra important to pre-heat your oven very thoroughly, as the more (cold) batter you are baking at once, the longer a cold oven takes to recover to its target baking temperature after loading.

Troubleshooting

This is not an exhaustive list but covers the most likely problems. And no, it's not cool to think up new ways to mess up that aren't on this list.

Cake never rises

- raising agents past their use-by date
- raising agents / acid were not weighed accurately (under-weighed)
- extra additions were added, weighing down the batter
- cake not baked immediately after mixing was finished
- oven too cold (or not pre-heated, or oven thermometer not used)

Cake rises but sinks in the middle (and surface cracked as a result)

- raising agents / acid were not weighed accurately (over-weighed)
- gluten-free flour used instead of gluten-based flour
- cake flour used instead of all-purpose or white spelt
- batter was under-mixed
- oven too hot (over-heated, oven thermometer not used)

Cake rises but is very domed (and surface cracked as a result)

- raising agents / acid were not weighed accurately (under-weighed)
- sugar wasn't dissolved sufficiently in wet mix
- oven too cold (or not pre-heated, or oven thermometer not used)
- oven too hot (over-heated, oven thermometer not being used)

Cake rises, and is flat, but is still cracked on top

- all-purpose flour was used instead of spelt
- sugar wasn't dissolved sufficiently in wet mix

Cake gummy in the middle

- raising agents / acid were not weighed accurately (under-weighed)
- granulated sugar was swapped for liquid sugar (syrup)
- extra additions were added, weighing down the batter
- oven too cold (or not pre-heated, or oven thermometer not used)
- oven fan speed lower than average (increase temp. to compensate)

Crumb too tight/ volume too small

- raising agents / acid were not weighed accurately (under-weighed)
- syrup was used instead of granulated sugar
- sugar was reduced from recipe level
- extra additions were added, weighing down the batter
- batter was overmixed
- oven too cold (or not pre-heated, or oven thermometer not used)

Cake too chewy/ too bready/ not tender enough

- flour with too high a gluten content was used (eg bread flour)
- pea protein was omitted or not weighed accurately
- syrup was used instead of granulated sugar
- sugar was reduced from recipe level
- fat/ oil level was reduced from recipe level
- batter was over-mixed

Crumb too open

- bicarbonate of soda was used instead of baking powder
- raising agents / acid were not weighed accurately (over-weighed)
- an acidic addition that wasn't in recipe has been added/ substituted

Cake too crumbly*

- gluten-free flour was used instead of gluten-based flour
- cake flour was used instead of all-purpose or white spelt
- extra fat/ oil was added, or not weighed correctly (over-weighed)
- batter was under-mixed
- *crumbliness always increases as a cake stales. To extend the shelf life of any of my cake recipes, replace half the pea protein with more flour, and replace half the plant milk with aquafaba. Be aware that there's a trade off involved; doing this will increase the stickiness and reduce the fluffiness of the cake on the day it's baked, and reduce the overall richness and sweetness of flavour*

Pockets of flour in the crumb

- flour contained lumps, and wasn't sieved before dry mixing
- batter under-mixed, or not mixed immediately after dry added to wet
- insufficient scraping down/ turning over of batter whilst mixing
- additions added in too early before flour fully hydrated in the batter

Cake tastes bitter, and/or slightly salty

- raising agents / acid were not weighed accurately (over-weighed)
- salt not weighed accurately (over-weighed)
- buckwheat flour used instead of all purpose flour or spelt

Sugar crystals on top or grainy/ crunchy in the crumb

- sugar was added into dry mix, instead of being dissolved in wet mix
- granulated sugar that was used was not fine enough
- wet mix was under-mixed, not dissolving the sugar

Cake too bland

- pea protein/ salt/ sugar/ essence omitted or under-weighed
- white sugar was used instead of golden caster sugar
- acidic element not weighed accurately (under-weighed)
- additions used were poor quality

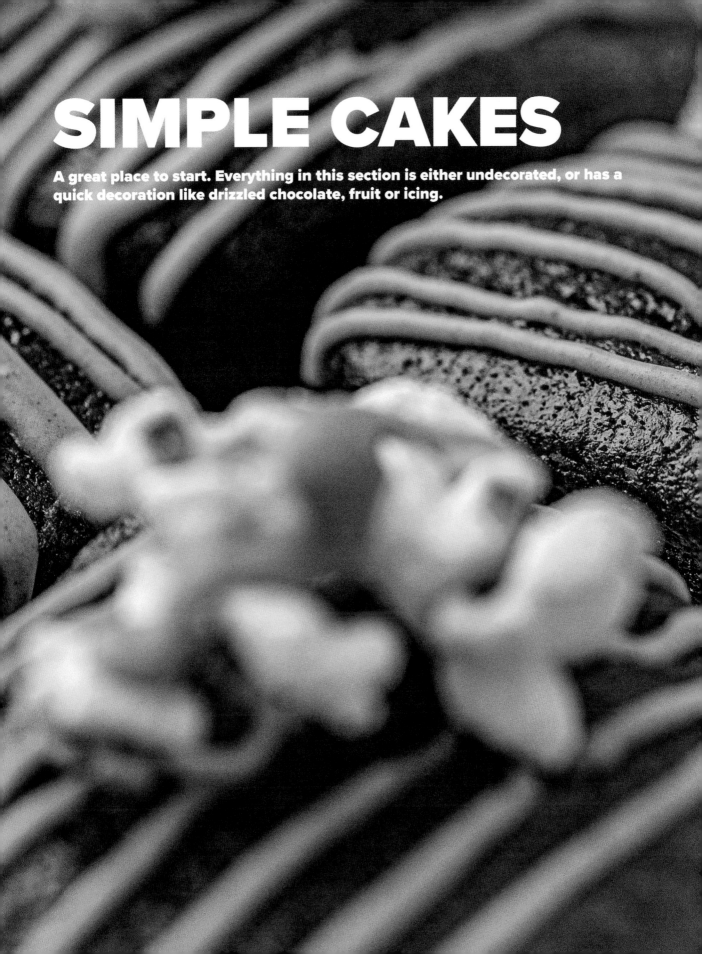

SIMPLE CAKES

A great place to start. Everything in this section is either undecorated, or has a quick decoration like drizzled chocolate, fruit or icing.

Mango & Pineapple Banana Bread

Key Kit	Approx Timings	
Hand mixer or stand mixer	Pre-baking	20
Oven thermometer	Baking	58-60 mins
1lb Loaf Tin	Decoration	-
	TOTAL	1 hr 20 mins
	(excluding cooling time)	

Makes	Storage & Shelf Life
1 loaf cake (6 portions)	Room temp. for 3 days

What to expect

This is still very much a Banana Bread, just with a summery twist. Adding the mango and pineapple make this a touch sweeter, without having to add extra sugar.

Hacks

Baking with coconut oil has become super-trendy in vegan baking in recent years, but unless you use a processed, deodorised version, it always gives a slight coconut flavour. I usually prefer using ingredients in their most natural state so usually steer clear of the deodorised version and only use coconut oil when the flavour really suits what I'm baking. Well, it **really** suits this one and beefs up the desiccated coconut flavour. If you don't like the taste of coconut, (or the price of coconut oil), then this still works if you substitute the coconut oil for sunflower oil, and the desiccated coconut for ground almonds.

Make

Get prepared

» This recipe is based on very ripe Bananas (with at least some brown spots on the skin)
» Weigh out the fruit from the Additions section now; you'll need those ready to add to your batter as soon as the mixing has finished. Chop into small pieces (so every slice of bread gets some fruit)
» Weigh and slice fruit from the Decoration section now as you want this ready to go straight onto the batter once it's in the tin
» Heat the oven to 155°C (311°F). Prepare a 1lb loaf tin ready with lightly greased baking paper
» You'll get much better results by baking your tin on a pre-heated **heavy** baking tray

Mix the Wet ingredients

» Mash Bananas thoroughly with a fork and set aside
» Weigh Coconut Oil into a small bowl and, if needed, sit the bowl in hot water to melt the Coconut Oil. Once melted, add Coconut Oil & Banana to a mixing bowl or stand mixer bowl. Weigh the other wet ingredients into the same bowl
» Use a whisk attachment (for a stand mixer) or a beater attachment (for a hand mixer), and mix on speed 3 for 8 minutes.
» The sugar should be partly dissolved by the end of this stage

Wet	g	oz
Peeled Bananas	214	7.5
Coconut Oil (melted)	50	1.8
Golden Caster Sugar	86	3.0
Apple Cider Vinegar	16	0.6
Vanilla Extract (ethanol)	5	0.2

Mix the Dry ingredients

» Weigh the Dry ingredients from Pea Protein down to Bicarbonate of Soda and pass through a sieve into another bowl. (The Desiccated Coconut won't go through the sieve).
» Now add the Desiccated Coconut and stir through to evenly distribute until the Dry ingredients are a uniform colour

Dry	g	oz
Pea Protein	18	0.6
White Spelt Flour	176	6.2
Sea Salt	2	0.1
Baking Powder	5	0.2
Ground Ginger	4	0.2
Bicarb. of Soda	3	0.1
Desiccated Coconut	44	1.5

Mix Wet & Dry together

» Use a hand mixer or a stand mixer with paddle attachment
» Add the Dry ingredients to the Wet and start mixing immediately
» Mix on speed 1 for 30 seconds
» The batter will seem super-thick but don't be tempted to add liquid at this stage. The Coconut "drinks" up a lot of the moisture (so it looks drier than it really is)

Mango & Pineapple Banana Bread

After mixing

» Add 50% of the dried fruit and stir through with a spatula
» Stirring should take about 15 seconds (don't over stir!)
» Add the remaining 50% of the fruit and stir again
» Tip your batter out into the greased tin. Level off with a spatula

Additions	g	oz
Dried Mango pieces	62	2.2
Dried Pineapple pieces	62	2.2

Decorate & Bake

» All weights in this section are approximate
» Slice banana 5mm (1/4 inch) thick, place on the long sides of the loaf. The weight is around 1 small banana cut in half
» Place pineapple in the middle of the loaf (this is the hottest part of the loaf where the banana might burn). Press the banana and pineapple slightly into the batter until it's almost flush. Bake
» Remove loaf from the oven when a toothpick or thin skewer comes out of the cake cleanly with (almost) no residue

Decoration	g	oz
Peeled Banana	130	4.6
Pineapple	23	0.8

Bake
155°C (311°F)
for 58 minutes

Walnut & Cinnamon Banana Bread
(gluten-free)

Key Kit
Hand mixer or stand mixer
Oven thermometer
1lb Loaf Tin

Makes
1 Loaf Cake (6 portions)

Approx Timings
Pre-baking	30 mins
Baking	53 mins
Decoration	-
TOTAL	83 mins

(excluding cooling time)

Storage & Shelf Life
Room temp. for 3 days

What to expect
A great way to use up over-ripe bananas, the walnut & cinnamon combination is a classic for good reason, and adding almond flour takes it to another level. As this is gluten free, you won't get big oven spring when baking it, but don't panic, you'll still get a lovely soft, moist crumb.

Hacks
Some of you will already know that you always get slightly less rise out of a gluten-free cake than a gluten-based one, and in general, it's much easier to get great results from small gluten-free cakes than big ones. The less expanded, less open batter means the heat struggles to penetrate to a cake's core, so there's a higher risk of a slightly gummy cake centre after baking. One of the hacks for this is to bake gluten-free cakes 5-10 degrees hotter than the gluten-based cakes. And it's **super**-important to pre-heat your oven fully before baking gluten-free loaf cakes.

Walnut & Cinnamon Banana Bread (gluten-free)

Make & Bake

Get prepared: *pre-heating your oven is extra important on this recipe
- » Heat the oven to 155°C (311°F). Prepare a 1lb loaf tin with lightly greased baking paper
- » Weigh the Walnuts (see "Additions") & toast in the oven for 8 mins at 155°C (311°F). Break in half
- » Weigh & slice Banana from "Decoration" section so it's ready to use as soon as the mixing is done
- » You'll get much better results by baking your tin on a pre-heated **heavy** baking tray

Mix the Wet ingredients
- » Mash very ripe Bananas with a fork. Put in mixing bowl or stand mixer bowl. Weigh the other Wet ingredients into the same bowl
- » Using a hand mixer, or a stand mixer with a whisk attachment, mix on speed 3 for 4 minutes
- » The sugar should be partly dissolved by the end of this stage

Wet	g	oz
Peeled Ripe Bananas	248	8.8
Sunflower Oil	47	1.7
White Caster Sugar	99	3.5
Apple Cider Vinegar	18	0.7
Vanilla Extract (ethanol)	6	0.2

Mix the Dry ingredients
- » Weigh & sieve all the Dry ingredients except Ground Almonds over another bowl. Add Ground Almonds to the sieved Dry ingredients and stir through thoroughly
- » Weigh Baking Powder and Bicarbonate of Soda into a separate bowl. *Make sure to keep these separate as they are added to the final mix at a different stage to the rest of the Dry ingredients
- » If you turned your oven off after toasting the nuts, switch it back on again at this stage so it's hot and ready to go

Dry	g	oz
Pea Protein	25	0.9
White Rice Flour	97	3.4
Sea Salt	2	0.1
Cinnamon	3	0.1
Arrowroot	25	0.9
Ground Almonds	97	3.4

Mix Wet & Dry together
- » Add the Dry ingredients to the Wet in your mixer bowl
- » Mix on speed 3 for 6 minutes using a hand mixer or a stand mixer with a paddle attachment
- » Add raising agents and mix speed 1 for 30 seconds

Raising Agents	g	oz
Baking Powder	6	0.2
Bicarb. of Soda	3	0.1

After mixing
- » In 2 stages, add the roasted nuts, stirring briefly after each stage
- » Tip your batter out into the greased tin. Level off with a wet palette knife or spatula (it doesn't have to be perfect)
- » Slice Banana 5mm (1/4 inch) thick, place on long sides of the loaf
- » Rinse Walnuts in water (this prevents them from burning) and place them between the banana slices on top of the cake
- » Press nuts and Banana slightly into the batter until almost flush
- » Bake until a toothpick comes out cleanly with (almost) no residue
- » Be prepared for this to take longer than the bake time given here

Additions	g	oz
Walnuts	84	3.0

Decoration	g	oz
Peeled Banana	67	2.4
Walnuts (soaked)	10	0.4

Bake
155°C (311°F) for 53 minutes+

Iced Lemon Loaf Cake

Key Kit
Hand mixer or stand mixer
Oven thermometer
1lb Loaf Tin

Makes
1 Loaf Cake (6 portions)

Approx Timings
Pre-baking	15-20 mins
Baking	68 mins
Decoration	5-10 mins
TOTAL	90-100 mins

(excluding cooling time)

Storage & Shelf Life
Room temperature for 3 days

What to expect
A simple plant-based version of a classic. Fresh and light with a lovely lemon zing. If you're tight for time or want a low-sugar option, bake it naked without the icing.

Hacks
Although I love using natural ingredients, I'm using lemon extract rather than the juice of fresh lemons here, because lemons vary hugely in their acidity. Some of the trial cakes I made were perfect, and some were much too sour, yet both used the same amount of fresh lemon juice. Using extract standardises things, (deeply pleasing my inner nerd) and is a more reliable way of achieving a balanced lemon flavour.

Quick heads-up: you need to pay attention to what type of extract you're using. Some are made by infusing oil, and others use ethanol. You can use either, but I've based the recipe on ethanol-based extract which is a little more expensive but more potent (so you need a lot less). To use oil-based extract there's a little hack you have to do (explained on the recipe itself).

Iced Lemon Loaf Cake

Make & Bake

Get prepared
» Zest your lemons to get the weight shown below. (You'll need around 2 large/ 3 small lemons)
» Check your Lemon Extract: if it's ethanol based, just use the recipe as it is. If it's oil-based, double the extract to 38g (1.3oz), and reduce the Sunflower Oil to 75g (2.6oz)
» Pre-heat the oven to 160°C (320°F). Line a one-pound baking tin with lightly greased baking paper
» You'll get much better results by baking your tin on a pre-heated **heavy** baking tray

Mix the Wet ingredients
» Weigh Wet ingredients into a mixing bowl or stand mixer bowl
» Using a hand mixer, or a stand mixer with a paddle attachment, mix on speed 3 for 6 minutes
» The Sugar should be partly dissolved by the end of this stage

Wet	g	oz
Lemon Extract (ethanol)	19	0.7
White Caster Sugar	253	8.9
Plant Milk of your choice	113	4.0
Apple Cider Vinegar	18	0.6
Lemon Zest	14	0.5
Sunflower Oil	113	4.0

Mix the Dry ingredients
» Weigh and sieve all the Dry ingredients over another bowl
» Stir through to evenly distribute (don't skip this step) until the Dry ingredients are a uniform colour

Dry	g	oz
Pea Protein	42	1.5
All Purpose Flour	167	5.9
Sea Salt	2	0.1
Baking Powder	3	0.1

Mix Wet & Dry together
» Set a timer ready with 30 seconds on the clock
» Add the Dry ingredients to the Wet in the mixing bowl
» Start mixing immediately and mix on speed 1 for 30 seconds

After mixing
» Using a spatula or scraper, tip batter out of bowl into your tin
» Smooth over using a palette knife or spatula. Bake
» Remove cake from the oven when a toothpick or thin skewer comes out of the cake cleanly with (almost) no residue
» Loaf cakes are sensitive to different ovens so check your loaf at 1 hour. You may need less or more time than my suggested 68 minutes

Bake
160°C (320°F)
for 68 minutes

Iced Lemon Loaf Cake

Decorate

Get prepared
» To get a solid or semi-solid glaze the cake must be room temperature or slightly above before icing
» If you don't mind a thinner, less opaque glaze, you can glaze when the cake is slightly warm
» Juice the lemons you have already zested to achieve the weight below
» If your lemons aren't juicy enough to achieve the weight in the recipe, top up using bottled lemon juice, but if you use 100% bottled lemon juice it will definitely not be as delicious.

Make the Icing
» Weigh the Icing Sugar into a small bowl and add the Lemon Juice
» Hand whisk until smooth-ish
» Place small bowl into a jug of hot water to melt
» Stir until it's smooth and very pourable
» Pour over your cake and finish with a sprinkle of grated Lemon Zest for some colour and extra lemon flavour

Icing	g	oz
Icing Sugar	130	4.6
Fresh Lemon Juice	24	0.9
Lemon Zest	3	0.1

Apple & Ginger Cake

Key Kit

Hand mixer or stand mixer
Oven thermometer
1 x 20cm Round (8 inch)

Makes

6 good-sized portions

Approx Timings

Pre-baking	30 mins
Baking	43-45 mins
Decoration	-
TOTAL	75 mins

(excluding cooling time)

Storage & Shelf Life

Room temp. for 3 days

What to expect

Perhaps the ultimate home-baked cake? Wholesome, natural, and full of fruit and spice. At Timberhill Bakery we made much fancier, richer, more indulgent cakes than this, but week in, week out, Summer or Winter, this cake was the best seller. It's that good.

Hacks

This shows how a really simple cake can taste amazing with the right ingredients. To achieve big apple flavour I've combined fresh apples and apple juice concentrate, and for the ginger flavour I've used grated fresh ginger **and** some crystallised ginger.

If you can't get apple juice concentrate you can substitute for another syrup, such as maple syrup and the cake's structure will be maintained; (it'll just have less apple flavour). Don't be tempted to sub the juice concentrate for apple juice - the batter will be too thin, and your cake might collapse. And on the ginger front, don't even think about using ground ginger instead - use fresh, it'll be worth it.

Apple & Ginger Cake

Make

Get prepared
» Dice the Additions Apple by hand into small pieces. (There's no need to peel the apples)
» Chop the Additions Crystallised Ginger into small pieces. Peel the Fresh Ginger and grate finely
» Prepare Decoration Apple at this stage so it's ready to use as soon as the mixing has finished
» Heat the oven to 160°C (320°F). Get a 20cm (8") round tin ready with lightly greased baking paper
» You'll get much better results by baking your tin on a pre-heated **heavy** baking tray

Mix the Wet ingredients
» Weigh Wet ingredients into a mixing bowl or stand mixer bowl
» Using a hand mixer or a stand mixer with a paddle attachment, mix on speed 2 for 3 minutes
» The Sugar should be partly dissolved by the end of this stage

Wet	g	oz
Plant Milk of your choice	107	3.8
Sunflower Oil	87	3.1
Apple Juice Concentrate	44	1.5
Fresh Ginger	26	0.9
Apple Cider Vinegar	17	0.6

Mix the Dry ingredients
» Weigh and sieve all Dry ingredients over another bowl
» You can substitute the Spelt flour with All Purpose if you prefer
» Stir through to evenly distribute (don't skip this step) until the Dry ingredients are a uniform colour

Dry	g	oz
White Spelt Flour	175	6.2
Sea Salt	2	pinch
Baking Powder	3	0.1
Bicarb. of Soda	2	pinch
Cinnamon	10	0.4
Demerara Sugar	87	3.1
White Caster Sugar	87	3.1
Pea Protein	44	1.5

Mix wet & dry together
» Set a timer ready with 30 seconds on the clock
» Add the Dry ingredients to the Wet in the mixing bowl
» Start mixing immediately and mix on speed 1 for 20 secs
» Scrape down with a spatula, (look out for apple juice concentrate stuck on the bottom of the bowl). Mix on speed 1 for 20 secs

After mixing
» Fold in Additions by hand with a spatula for around 20 seconds
» Tip out into your lined and greased round tin, and level off with an offset spatula. Go straight onto the next stage, with no delay

Additions	g	oz
Apple	134	4.7
Crystallised Ginger	43	1.5

Apple & Ginger Cake

Decorate & Bake

» All weights in this section are approximate

» Slice apple thinly and cover about two thirds of the top of the cake. Be sure not to use very thick slices of apple or the apple will weigh down the batter too much and inhibit the rise a little

» Bake. Remove the cake from the oven when a toothpick comes out of the cake cleanly

Decoration	g	oz
Apple	91	3.2

Bake
160°C (320°F)
for 43 minutes

Apricot & Pecan Breakfast Muffins

Key Kit
Hand mixer or stand mixer
Oven thermometer
Muffin tin, tulip cases

Approx Timings
Pre-baking	20-25 mins
Baking	23 mins
Decoration	-
TOTAL	42-47 mins

(excluding cooling time)

Makes
6 muffins

Storage & Shelf Life
Room temp. for 3 days

What to expect
A quick-to-make breakfast treat, or a well-behaved snack when you're in the mood for nuts & fruit rather than chocolate. Coconut sugar is perfect for this, giving an extra layer of flavour despite the lower sugar level.

Hacks
Coconut Sugar has an amazing ability to absorb liquid, so compared to other muffins in this book, I've increased the Plant Milk and reduced the baking time to nail the crumb texture I wanted.

You can substitute with another kind of sugar providing you add 3-5 minutes to the bake time, and don't mind a slightly sticky crumb and a flat top (rather than a dome) to your muffins. Either way, they'll still taste great. Other substitutions include: swapping the pecans for another nut (another light, soft nut like walnuts works best), changing the apricots to raisins or cranberries, or switching the subtle level of ground ginger for cinnamon.

Apricot & Pecan Breakfast Muffins

Make & Bake

Get prepared
» Toast Pecans in the oven for around 8 minutes at around 160°C (320°F). Once toasted break the Pecans in half. Weigh out the Apricots from the "Additions" section, and set aside
» Prepare your muffin tin and cases so they are ready. Pre-heat the oven to 170°C (338°F)
» Check your Orange Extract: if it's ethanol based, just use the recipe as it is. If it's oil-based, double the extract to 16g (0.6oz), and reduce the Sunflower Oil to 87g (3.1oz)

Mix the Wet ingredients
» Weigh Wet ingredients into a mixing bowl or stand mixer bowl
» Using a hand mixer, or a stand mixer with a whisk attachment, mix on speed 3 for 6 minutes

Wet	g	oz
Almond Milk	183	6.5
Sunflower Oil	103	3.7
Orange Extract (ethanol)	8	0.3
Apple Cider Vinegar	21	0.7
Coconut Sugar	191	6.8

Mix the Dry ingredients
» Weigh and sieve all the Dry ingredients over another bowl
» Stir through to evenly distribute until the Dry ingredients are a uniform colour

Dry	g	oz
White Spelt Flour	193	6.8
Sea Salt	2	0.1
Ground Ginger	11	0.4
Pea Protein	52	1.8
Baking Powder	10	0.4
Bicarb. of Soda	2	0.1

Mix Wet & Dry together
» Add the Dry ingredients to the Wet into your mixer bowl
» Using a hand mixer, or stand mixer with paddle attachment, start mixing immediately on speed 1 for 30 seconds

After mixing
» Add the Pecans & Apricots into the batter & stir briefly (20 secs)
» Scoop batter into muffin cases; approx 143g each (5.1oz)
» Turn batter over whilst scooping to distribute everything evenly

Additions	g	oz
Dried Apricots (diced)	77	2.7
Pecans	77	2.7

Decoration & Baking
» Sprinkle Flaked Almonds on top of the muffins before baking
» Bake until a skewer comes out of the muffin cleanly

Decoration	g	oz
Flaked Almonds	29	1.0

Bake
170°C (338°F) for 30 minutes

Peanut Butter, Banana & Chocolate Muffins

Key Kit
Hand mixer or stand mixer
Oven thermometer
Muffin tin, tulip cases

Makes
6 muffins

Approx Timings
Pre-baking	30
Baking	30 mins
Decoration	1 min
TOTAL	60-65 mins

(excluding cooling time)

Storage & Shelf Life
Room temp. for 3 days

What to expect
Expect **everybody** to love them. Literally everyone. Even people who don't really like peanut butter, or banana. (And I've never met anyone who doesn't like chocolate).

Hacks
Two little hacks make a big difference on this recipe. The first is using olive oil for 20% of the total oil, and the second is using molasses syrup for just 6% of the total sugar. If you've run out of olive oil you can substitute with extra sunflower oil, and if you can't get molasses syrup then maple syrup is a good stand-in.

Both substitutions will allow the muffins to rise just as well and keep their structure. They'll still be great; they just won't get nabbed **quite** as quickly.

Make & Bake

Get prepared
» Mash Bananas thoroughly with a fork and set aside. Weigh Additions Chocolate and dice into chips
» Weigh Decoration Chocolate and melt this in a small bowl over another bowl of boiling water
» Get your muffin tin and cases trayed up and ready. Heat the oven to 170°C (338°F)

Mix the Wet ingredients

» Weigh Wet ingredients into a mixing bowl or stand mixer bowl
» Using a hand mixer, or a stand mixer with a whisk attachment, mix on speed 3 for 6 minutes
» The Sugar should be partly dissolved by the end

Wet	g	oz
Peeled Bananas	135	4.7
Demerara Sugar	202	7.1
Almond Milk	93	3.3
Apple Cider Vinegar	18	0.6
Sunflower Oil	67	2.4
Olive Oil	17	0.6
Peanut Butter	84	3.0
Molasses Syrup	13	0.4

Mix the Dry ingredients

» Weigh and sieve all the Dry ingredients over another bowl
» Stir through to evenly distribute (don't skip this step) until the Dry ingredients are a uniform colour

Dry	g	oz
Pea Protein	21	0.7
White Spelt Flour	118	4.2
Sea Salt	2	0.1
Baking Powder	8	0.3

Mix Wet & Dry together
» Add the Dry ingredients to the Wet into your mixer bowl
» Using a hand mixer, or stand mixer with paddle attachment, start mixing immediately on speed 1 for 30 seconds

After mixing

» In 2 stages, tip Chocolate Chips into batter & stir briefly (20 secs)
» Scoop batter into muffin cases; approx 140g each (4.9oz)
» Turn batter over whilst scooping to distribute Choc Chips evenly

Additions	g	oz
Choc Chips (vegan)	100	3.5

Decoration & Baking

» Drizzle melted Chocolate Chips on top of muffins before baking
» Zig-zag across the muffin and swirl through with a skewer
» Bake until a skewer comes out of the muffin cleanly

Decoration	g	oz
Choc Chips (vegan)	23	0.4

Bake
170°C (338°F)
for 30 minutes

Lemon & Raspberry Ripple Muffins

Key Kit

Hand mixer or stand mixer
Oven thermometer
Silicone mould/ tulip cases

Makes

6 Muffins

Approx Timings

Pre-baking	20 mins
Baking	30 mins
Decoration	10 mins
TOTAL	60 mins

(excluding cooling time)

Storage & Shelf Life

Room temp. for 3 days

What to expect

Another big seller from Timberhill Bakery and a simple way to bake something delicious **and** really pretty. Tight-ish, moist crumb, with a great combination of lemon & raspberry. Can also be baked in tulip cases.

Hacks

In general, smaller cakes take additions so much better than larger cakes that you can even add fruit smooshes in the middle of the batter and they'll still bake well. The faster penetration of heat to the centre of a small cake means the smoosh doesn't cause a soggy core like it would in a loaf cake.

I've also squeezed almond into this recipe by replacing a fifth of the flour for ground almonds. At this level of substitution (15-20%), the structure of the cake is unaffected and the crumb becomes even more moist.

Lemon & Raspberry Ripple Muffins

Make & Bake

Get prepared
» Weigh out the Raspberries. If using Fresh Raspberries, smoosh them by crushing with a fork (or use a food processor) until smooth. Transfer to a bowl or squeezy bottle and set aside
» If using Frozen Raspberries, take out of the freezer and smoosh (from frozen) in a blender until smooth. Transfer to a bowl or squeezy bottle and sit it in a jug of hot water to defrost until pourable
» Zest your lemons to achieve the weight shown below. (You'll need around 2 large/ 3 small lemons)
» Check your Lemon Extract: if it's ethanol based, just use the recipe as it is. If it's oil-based, double the extract to 36g (1.3oz), and reduce the Sunflower Oil to 60g (2.1oz)
» Heat the oven to 170°C (338°F). Use a fluted silicone baking mould and grease with non-stick spray
» (If you haven't got fluted moulds you can make regular muffins with tulip cases with this recipe)

Mix the Wet ingredients
» Weigh Wet ingredients into a mixing bowl or stand mixer bowl
» Using a hand mixer or a stand mixer with a paddle attachment, mix on speed 3 for 6 minutes
» The Sugar should be partly dissolved by the end

Wet	g	oz
Lemon Extract (ethanol)	18	0.6
White Caster Sugar	217	7.6
Almond Milk	93	3.3
Apple Cider Vinegar	15	0.5
Lemon Zest	12	0.4
Sunflower Oil	96	3.4

Mix the Dry ingredients
» Sieve all the Dry ingredients from Pea Protein down to Baking Powder over another bowl (Ground Almonds won't sieve)
» Add the Ground Almonds and stir through to evenly distribute (don't skip this step) until the Dry ingredients are a uniform colour

Dry	g	oz
Pea Protein	39	1.4
White Spelt Flour	123	4.4
Sea Salt	2	0.1
Baking Powder	3	0.1
Ground Almonds	21	0.8

Mix Wet & Dry together
» Set a timer ready with 30 seconds on the clock
» Add the Dry ingredients to the Wet in the mixing bowl
» Start mixing immediately and mix on speed 1 for 30 seconds

After mixing
» Scoop or spoon a quarter of the batter into each mould first
» Add a thick swirl of smooshed Raspberries on top
» Repeat twice (so 3 layers of batter and Raspberries)
» Finish up with some cake batter on top
» Bake immediately, until a toothpick comes out clean

Additions	g	oz
Raspberries	72	2.5

Bake
170°C (338°F)
for 30 minutes

Lemon & Raspberry Ripple Muffins

Decorate

Get prepared

» To get a solid or semi-solid glaze the cake must be room temperature or slightly above before icing
» If you don't mind a thinner, less opaque glaze, you can glaze the cakes when they're slightly warm
» Juice the Lemons you've already zested to get the weight below. Top up using bottled lemon juice if you're short of the weight, (but if you use 100% bottled lemon juice it definitely won't be as delicious)
» Prepare a small jug of very hot water which you'll use to melt the icing before pouring onto the cake

Make the Icing

» Weigh the Icing Sugar into a small bowl and add the Lemon Juice
» Hand whisk until smooth-ish and place the small bowl into your jug of hot water to melt. Stir until it's smooth and very pourable
» Pour over your cake and finish with a sprinkle of grated Lemon Zest or Raspberries for some colour and extra flavour

Icing	g	oz
Icing Sugar	156	5.5
Fresh Lemon Juice	29	1.0
Lemon Zest	5	0.2
(or Raspberries)		

Apple Hedgerow Mini Loaf

(gluten-free)

Key Kit
Hand mixer or stand mixer
Oven thermometer
8 loaf mini loaf tin

Approx Timings
Pre-baking	30 mins
Baking	33 mins
Decoration	10 - 12 mins
TOTAL	75 mins

(excluding cooling time)

Makes
8 mini loaf cakes

Storage & Shelf Life
Room temp. for 3 days

What to expect
A cake that packs in the fresh fruits and isn't frightened to use super-sharp fruits like Granny Smiths and blackberries. Hearty and wholesome feel.

Hacks
You may have noticed that the first mix is very long and fast on these cakes. When you bake with gluten-free flours, you can mix much longer with no risk of a chewy crumb developing. Also, ground almonds can give a slightly grainy crumb, so a long mix time can be used to soften them helping to give a less coarse batter.

However, adding the raising agents at the start of this long mix would mean they'd run out of raising power before the cake was baked (giving less rise). That's why the raising agents are held back until the first mix is complete. That fast and long first mix time, combined with a short, slow, second mix is the key here.

Make & Bake

Get prepared
» Wash and drain Blackberries thoroughly. Chop large berries into two, leave medium ones whole
» Dice the Apple from the "Additions" section by hand into small pieces
» Prepare your mini-loaf tin with non-stick baking spray, and preheat your oven to 165°C (330°F)

Weigh the Wet ingredients
» Weigh Wet ingredients into a mixing bowl or stand mixer bowl

Wet	g	oz
Almond Milk	208	7.4
Sunflower Oil	61	2.2
Apple Juice Concentrate	61	2.2
Vanilla Extract (ethanol)	10	0.4
Apple Cider Vinegar	25	0.9

Weigh the Dry ingredients
» Weigh all the Dry ingredients and stir through to evenly distribute, until they are a uniform colour
» There's no need to sieve these ingredients with this recipe

Dry	g	oz
White Rice Flour	139	4.9
Sea Salt	2	1/2 tsp
Cinnamon	15	0.5
Pea Protein	31	1.1
White Caster Sugar	245	8.7
Arrowroot	31	1.1
Ground Almonds	139	4.9

Mix Wet & Dry together
» Add the Dry ingredients to the Wet in your mixing bowl
» Using a hand mixer or a stand mixer with a paddle attachment, mix on speed 3 for 10 minutes

Raising Agents
» Add Baking Powder & Bicarbonate of Soda into the mixing bowl
» Using a hand mixer or a stand mixer with a paddle attachment, mix on speed 1 for 40 seconds

Dry (cont)	g	oz
Baking Powder	5	0.2
Bicarb. of Soda	1	pinch

After mixing
» Using a spatula, stir through the additions by hand
» Divide batter evenly between cakes (approx 145g (5.1oz) each)

» Bake immediately, until a toothpick comes out clean
» Allow to cool for 1-2 hours before decorating

Additions	g	oz
Blackberries	118	4.2
Apple	129	4.5

Bake
165°C (330°F)
for 33 minutes

Decorate

Make the Icing

» Weigh Icing Sugar into a jug (or food processor) and add whole Blackberries
» Whisk (or blend) until smooth (approx 3 mins), scraping down regularly, ensuring everything is incorporated
» Scrape out into either a squeezy bottle or small jug. Using a squeezy bottle makes it easier to drizzle on the icing but you may need to sieve the icing after blending, to remove the pips which can get stuck in the nozzle of the bottle
» To make the icing runny enough to drizzle, warm it first by putting your jug or squeezy bottle in a jug of hot water
» Drizzle the icing on the cakes
» Sprinkle Icing Sugar on top, and finish with Blackberries

Icing	g	oz
Icing Sugar	109	3.8
Blackberries	28	1.0

Finishing	g	oz
Icing Sugar	7	0.2
Blackberries	35	1.2

Triple Ginger Gingerbread Mini Loaf

Key Kit	Approx Timings	
Hand mixer or stand mixer	Pre-baking	20 mins
Oven thermometer	Baking	28 mins
8 loaf mini loaf tin	Decoration	10 mins
	TOTAL	58 mins
	(excluding cooling time)	

Makes
8 mini loaf cakes

Storage & Shelf Life
Room temp. for 3 days

What to expect
Deeply sweet, slightly sticky and extremely gingery. Looks ordinary, tastes anything but. My kind of thing.

Hacks
The muscovado sugar and molasses syrup are the hacks to giving this cake its sticky, deep, distinctive sweetness, so it's worth the faff to seek these out. I've also used dried prunes, which might sound a bit weird, but they amp up that deep flavour and, combined with the crystallised ginger, provide some texture. These cakes are super high on the ginger scale so if you like things spicy, you'll love them as they are. If you want to dial things back a notch, then substitute the crystallised ginger for extra chopped prunes. Knock it back another notch again by substituting the ground ginger for more cinnamon. Whatever you do, don't substitute the fresh ginger - it adds so much more than just heat. Finally, a little hack on the drizzle; matching the icing colour to the popcorn (as I've done here) needs a little food colouring adding to it. Or, skip the icing altogether and use a shop-bought caramel or even ginger syrup for a lazy option.

Triple Ginger Gingerbread Mini Loaf

Make & Bake

Get prepared
» Peel and grate Fresh Ginger very finely
» Dice the Crystallised Ginger into small pieces, and the Prunes into quarters/ thirds
» Prepare your mini-loaf tin with non-stick baking spray, and preheat your oven to 160°C (320°F)
» Tip: wear an apron or use a deep mixing bowl as this one likes to splash around a bit

Weigh the Wet ingredients
» Weigh Wet ingredients into deep mixing bowl or stand mixer bowl
» If Muscovado is compacted, break up by hand as you weigh out
» Using a hand mixer or a stand mixer with a paddle attachment, mix on speed 3 for 2 minutes
» Scrape any Ginger off the paddle/ beater arms and mix again on speed 3 for 1 minute. The sugar should be partly dissolved

Wet	g	oz
Fresh Ginger	40	1.4
Sunflower Oil	100	3.5
Muscovado Sugar	100	3.5
Molasses Syrup	36	1.3
Maple Syrup	200	7.0
Apple Cider Vinegar	12	0.4
Plant Milk of your choice	170	6.0

Weigh the Dry ingredients
» Weigh and sieve all the Dry ingredients and stir through to evenly distribute, until they are a uniform colour

Dry	g	oz
White Spelt Flour	170	6.0
Pea Protein	50	1.8
Sea Salt	3	0.1
Baking Powder	2	0.1
Bicarb. of Soda	3	0.1
Cinnamon	13	0.4
Ground Ginger	13	0.4

Mix Wet & Dry together
» Add the Dry ingredients to the Wet in your mixing bowl
» Start mixing as soon as possible after adding in the Dry
» Mix on speed 1 for 20 seconds, scrape down
» Mix again on speed 1 for another 20 seconds

After mixing
» Using a spatula, stir through the Prunes & Crystallised Ginger
» Divide batter evenly between cakes (approx 120g (4.2oz) each
» Stir before each scoop to ensure every cake has an equal amount of Additions
» Bake immediately, until a toothpick comes out clean
» Allow to cool for 1-2 hours before decorating

Additions	g	oz
Prunes	65	2.3
Crystallised Ginger	65	2.3

Bake
160°C (320°F)
for 28 minutes

Decorate

Make the Icing

» Weigh Icing Sugar into a jug and add hot water & spices
» Whisk until very smooth (it normally takes a couple of minutes)
» Scrape out into either a squeezy bottle if you want to make it easier to drizzle the icing precisely, or use a spoon or spatula straight from the jug instead
» To make the icing runny enough to drizzle, warm it first by putting your jug or squeezy bottle in a jug of hot water
» Drizzle Icing on the cakes and finish with Popcorn

Icing	g	oz
Icing Sugar	116	4.1
Water (hot)	19	0.7
Ground Ginger	2	0.1
Cinnamon	1	pinch
Food Colouring (optional)		

Finishing	g	oz
Popcorn	by eye	by eye

Mango & Passion Fruit Mini Loaf

Key Kit
Hand mixer or stand mixer
Oven thermometer
8 loaf mini loaf tin

Makes
8 mini loaf cakes

Approx Timings
Pre-baking	20 mins
Baking	28 mins
Decoration	5 mins
TOTAL	53 mins
(excluding cooling time)	

Storage & Shelf Life
Chilled for 3 days

What to expect
One of the most moist cakes in this book, with a fruity mango crumb, creamy mango chunks and texture from the desiccated coconut. I've topped this cake with natural vegan yoghurt rather than an icing or frosting, to complement the amazingly tart passion fruit used to decorate it.

Hacks
As this cake's at the lighter, fresher end of the spectrum, I've used the trick from my cupcake recipes to engineer in some fluffiness to the crumb, by substituting half the pea protein with arrowroot. The slight loss of richness from a lower pea protein level is more than offset in this cake, as most of the plant milk I'd normally use is replaced with super-fruity mango pulp.

Finally, not everyone wants a cake with icing or frosting so I though this one would be a good candidate for a yoghurt topping (thicker yoghurts work best). If you want to push the sweetness further, you can use the icing from the Lemon Loaf Cake recipe for extra indulgence.

Mango & Passion Fruit Mini Loaf Cakes

Make & Bake

Get prepared
» Chop Mango Additions into almond-sized pieces. If using frozen Mango allow to defrost first
» Prepare your mini-loaf tin with non-stick baking spray, and preheat your oven to 160°C (320°F)

Weigh the Wet ingredients
» Weigh Wet ingredients into a mixing bowl or stand mixer bowl
» Check your Orange Extract: if it's ethanol based, just use the recipe as it is. If it's oil-based, double the extract to 22g (0.8oz) and reduce the Sunflower Oil to 74g (2.6oz)
» Using a hand mixer or a stand mixer with a paddle attachment, mix on speed 3 for 6 minutes until the sugar partly dissolves

Wet	g	oz
Mango Pulp (canned)	139	4.9
Plant Milk of your choice	54	1.9
Sunflower Oil	96	3.4
Orange Extract (ethanol)	11	0.4
Apple Cider Vinegar	21	0.8
Golden Caster Sugar	193	6.8

Weigh the Dry ingredients
» Weigh and sieve the Dry ingredients except Desiccated Coconut
» Add the Desiccated Coconut
» Stir through to evenly distribute, until a uniform colour

Dry	g	oz
White Spelt Flour	171	6.0
Sea Salt	2	pinch
Pea Protein	27	0.9
Arrowroot	27	0.9
Bicarb. of Soda	2	pinch
Baking Powder	11	0.4
Desiccated Coconut	75	2.6

Mix Wet & Dry together
» Add the Dry ingredients to the Wet in your mixing bowl
» Start mixing as soon as possible after adding in the Dry
» Mix on speed 1 for 20 seconds, scrape down
» Mix again on speed 1 for another 20 seconds

After mixing
» Using a spatula, stir through the Mango pieces by hand
» Divide batter evenly between cakes (approx 120g (4.2oz) each)
» Stir batter after each scooping to evenly distribute mango pieces
» Bake immediately, until a toothpick comes out clean
» Allow to cool for 1-2 hours before decorating

Additions	g	oz
Mango (fresh or frozen)	227	8.0

Bake
160°C (320°F)
for 28 minutes

Decorate
» Using the back of a spoon, spread the Yoghurt on the cakes
» Finish off with some fresh Passion Fruit to taste

	g	oz
Plant Yoghurt	200	7.1
Fresh Passion Fruit	80	2.8

Fudgy

HACKING THE PERFECT BROWNIE

Cakey, fudgy or somewhere in-between?

Cakey

Make *your* perfect brownie

Everyone has their own idea of what makes the perfect brownie, so in this section I'll show you how to make three different types, and you can decide for yourself which one's right for you.

Cakey

The first type is a Cakey Brownie which is like a very moist, more concentrated and dense chocolate cake. It uses a similar method to most of the cake recipes in this book with a few tweaks, the biggest of which is the ratio of wet ingredients to dry.

With a much wetter batter than any of my cake recipes, and therefore less toughness to worry about, the mixing times are slightly longer. This helps the cocoa powder to fully hydrate (avoiding a powdery mouth-feel) and fully develop a chocolatey flavour.

Fudgy

I've tasted a **lot** of brownies over the years and most have been delicious. The only time I'm really disappointed is when a brownie is described as having a "fudgy" texture when it's actually just a bit soggy and under-baked. So for this recipe I was determined to find a method of achieving extremely moist, smooth brownies without the soggy-ness.

The method I arrived at is more complex than my Cakey Brownie but the extra effort really pays off. This recipe took 22 attempts to perfect by testing different ways of binding, different fats and different sugars, and the final recipe is one of my favourites in this book.

Neither Pea Protein nor Aquafaba alone make a perfect fudgy brownie

My tests found that binding a very wet brownie with just pea protein gives amazing flavour, but the texture is a little too close to cakey.

Using aquafaba on its own instead gives a more gooey mouth-feel, but hitting the fudgy-ness sweet spot is very tricky. Drier aquafaba brownies have a slightly claggy mouth-feel, and wetter ones tip over into being over-soggy. This needs a new approach.

Combining Pea Protein **and** Aquafaba gives gooey without the soggy

Using a combination of both works wonders. Pea protein brings a depth of flavour and, being so effective at absorbing moisture, prevents soggy-ness. Aquafaba improves the mouth-feel, bringing a smooth gooey-ness. One without the other is nowhere near as good as the two combined.

The traditional whipping method helps achieve creamy mouth-feel

The mixing method also makes a big difference to the mouth-feel of Fudgy Brownies. With such a high ratio of fat, sugar and chocolate, a simple Wet & Dry method causes everything to separate slightly, adding to the dreaded sogginess. Longer mixing doesn't solve this and still leaves a slightly furry, cotton-wool-like texture.

The solution is to steal the method from eggs-and-butter cakes. If you think of aquafaba as similar to an egg-white, and pea protein as like an egg-yolk, this recipe essentially contains both elements of whole eggs.

As a result, aquafaba, pea protein and sugar can be whipped together, before the remainder of the other ingredients are added. This gives much better incorporation of the sugars, fats and dry ingredients, and a truly outstanding creamy, super-indulgent mouth-feel.

Oil, not plant butter, for the shiny crackle top

The main factor that influences crust is the fat used. Using oil rather than plant-based butter helps achieve a lovely shiny crust and the type of oil used also matters. Whilst coconut oil gives a shiny crust, it creates an overly dark crumb and a furry mouth-feel. Olive oil however, yields a perfect crumb colour, lovely indulgent mouth-feel **and** that crackle top.

Gluten-free

From my gluten-free flour cake trials, I knew I loved the texture of cakes made with buckwheat. However, there's no polite way of saying this, but buckwheat has an unpleasant, bitter flavour. I've seen this labelled as "earthy", but for me it's not suitable for cakes with a subtle flavour.

However, with a ton of chocolate, fat and sugar here, the bitter flavour is totally undetectable, so the Hazelnut Caramel Brownie in this section uses buckwheat and strikes a great midpoint between cakey and fudgy.

Chocolate Orange Cakey Brownies

Key Kit
Hand mixer or stand mixer
Oven thermometer
9" (23cm) Brownie Pan

Makes
12 small (or 9 big) Brownies

Approx Timings
Pre-baking	22 mins
Baking	28 mins
Decoration	-
TOTAL	40 mins

(excluding cooling time)

Storage & Shelf Life
Room temp. for 3 days

What to expect
Not as fudgy as the Fudgy Brownie recipe, but just as indulgent, and much easier and quicker to make. The tried-and-tested classic combo of chocolate and orange is loved by everyone, so reach for this recipe when you need something delicious in a hurry.

Hacks
A few tweaks can turn this into something even more indulgent that could be served as an after-dinner dessert. You can sub the orange extract for Grand Marnier (which is vegan), use orange sugar instead of demerara, and serve warm chunks of it with orange sorbet.

You can fine-tune this to make it a little more cakey (drier and fluffier), or slightly more fudgy (moist and dense) by changing the bake time. A couple of extra minutes makes it a little cakier, and a couple less minutes a smidge fudgier.

Chocolate Orange Cakey Brownies

Make & Bake

Get prepared
» Prepare a 23cm (9") Brownie tin lined with lightly greased baking paper
» If using a chocolate bar rather than drops, chop the Chocolate from Additions section into big chips
» Heat the oven to 180°C (355°F) with a pre-heated **heavy** baking tray inside. You'll need around 3 oranges, but zest and juice to get the exact weights of the recipe. Slice oranges for the decoration.

Mix the Wet ingredients
» Melt Chocolate Chips in a bowl sitting in another bowl of hot water. Stir through as they are melting

» Add all Wet ingredients (except the melting Chocolate Chips) into a mixing bowl or stand mixer bowl
» Using a hand mixer or stand mixer with paddle attachment, mix on speed 3 for 6 minutes, until the sugar is partially dissolved
» Add the melted Chocolate Chips into the same mixing bowl and mix on speed 3 for 2 minutes

Wet Mix	g	oz
Chocolate Chips	29	1.0
Olive Oil	210	7.4
Orange Juice	175	6.2
White Caster Sugar	187	6.6
Demerara Sugar	93	3.3
Orange Zest	12	0.4
Orange Extract (ethanol)	12	0.4

Dry Mix
» Weigh the Baking Powder and keep separate (this is added to the mix at a later stage than the other Dry ingredients)
» Weigh and sieve all the other Dry ingredients into another bowl
» Stir through by hand to ensure the ingredients are evenly distributed. The mixture should be a uniform colour by the end

Dry	g	oz
Baking Powder	7	0.3
White Spelt Flour	161	5.7
Sea Salt	6	0.2
Cocoa Powder (dutch)	29	1.0
Pea Protein	76	2.7

Mix Wet & Dry together
» Add Dry ingredients (exc Baking Powder) to the Wet in the mixing bowl and start mixing immediately on speed 1 for 45 seconds
» Quickly scrape down and mix again on speed 1 for 45 seconds
» Add Baking Powder and mix on speed 1 for 30 seconds

After mixing
» Add half the Chocolate Chips and stir through by hand using a spatula for about 20 seconds. Add the other half and stir again
» Tip out the mixture into your Brownie tin. The mixture will seem quite thick at this stage. Level off with an offset palette knife
» Place Orange Slices on top. Bake for 28 mins or until a toothpick comes out almost clean (perfectly clean gives a cakier brownie)

Additions	g	oz
Chocolate Chips	178	6.3
Orange Slices (approx)	12	0.4

Bake
180°C (355°F)
for 28 minutes

Fudgy Brownies

Key Kit
Hand mixer or stand mixer
Oven thermometer
9" (23cm) Brownie Pan

Approx Timings
Pre-baking	33 mins
Baking	27 mins
Decoration	-
TOTAL	1 hr
(excluding cooling time)	

Makes
12 small (or 9 big) Brownies

Storage & Shelf Life
Room temp. for 3 days

What to expect
This Brownie achieves that hard-to-hit sweet spot, between too cakey and too soggy. Incredibly moist with a very smooth texture. Super-indulgent in every way.

Hacks
If you're using a chocolate bar rather than chocolate chips make sure to chop it into good-sized chunks, (somewhere between hazelnut-sized and Brazil nut-sized). This prevents the chocolate from melting into the batter, which means you'll still get lovely pockets of melted chocolate in your brownie.

Substitutions: this is the best recipe in the book for a simple conversion to gluten-free. Just swap the spelt for buckwheat and you'll get almost identical results as the strong, slightly bitter flavour of Buckwheat doesn't get a look-in with this much chocolate.

I know this method looks like a bit of a faff compared to other 'amazing' brownie recipes out there. The difference? This one is the real deal.

Fudgy Brownies

Make

Get prepared
» Prepare a 23cm (9") Brownie tin lined with lightly greased baking paper
» If using a chocolate bar rather than drops, chop the Chocolate from Additions section into big chips
» Heat the oven to 170°C (340°F) with a pre-heated **heavy** baking tray inside

Mix the Wet ingredients

Wet Mix	g	oz
Chocolate Chips	29	1.0
Vanilla Extract (ethanol)	8	0.3
Plant Milk of your choice	58	2.0
Aquafaba	115	4.1
Pea Protein	75	2.6
White Caster Sugar	219	7.7
Demerara Sugar	58	2.0
Olive Oil	207	7.3

» Melt Chocolate Chips and Vanilla in a bowl sitting in another bowl of hot water. Stir through as they are melting

» Add Plant Milk and Aquafaba into a mixing bowl. Using a hand mixer or stand mixer with whisk, mix on speed 4 for 3 minutes

» Add the Pea Protein into the same mixing bowl
» Mix on speed 4 for 3 minutes

» Add all the Sugar into the same mixing bowl
» Mix on speed 4 for 3 minutes

» Drizzle the Olive Oil gradually into the same mixing bowl whilst mixing on speed 4 for 3 minutes

» Add the melted Chocolate and Vanilla into the same mixing bowl
» Mix on speed 4 for 2 minutes

Mix the Dry ingredients

Dry	g	oz
Baking Powder	8	0.3
White Spelt Flour	153	5.4
Sea Salt	6	0.2
Cocoa Powder (dutch)	29	1.0
Ground Coffee	6	0.2

» Weigh the Baking Powder and keep separate (this is added to the mix at a later stage than the other Dry ingredients)
» Sieve other Dry ingredients excluding Coffee over another bowl
» You can substitute the Spelt with All Purpose flour if you prefer
» Add the Ground Coffee and stir through to evenly distribute, until the Dry ingredients are a uniform colour

Mix Wet & Dry together
» If using a stand mixer change attachment from whisk to paddle
» Add Dry ingredients (exc Baking Powder) to the Wet in the mixing bowl and start mixing immediately on speed 1 for 45 seconds
» Quickly scrape down and mix again on speed 1 for 45 seconds
» Add Baking Powder and mix on speed 1 for 30 seconds

Bake

After mixing	Additions	g	oz
» Add half the Chocolate Chips and stir through by hand using a spatula for about 20 seconds	**Chocolate Chips**	**171**	6.0
» Add the remaining Chocolate Chips and stir through again			
» Tip out the mixture into your Brownie tin			
» Level off with an offset palette knife			
» The mixture will seem quite thick at this stage (this is normal)	**Bake**		
» Bake immediately for 27 mins or until a toothpick comes out almost clean (totally clean will give you a slightly cakier brownie)	**170°C (340°F)** for 27 minutes		

Hazelnut Caramel Buckwheat Brownies

(gluten-free)

Key Kit	Approx Timings	
Hand mixer or stand mixer	Pre-baking	30 mins
Oven thermometer	Baking	27 mins
9" (23cm) brownie pan	Decoration	20 mins
Thermometer for caramel	TOTAL	77 mins
	(excluding cooling time)	

Makes	Storage & Shelf Life
12 small (or 9 big) Brownies	Chilled for 3 days

What to expect

A nutty, rich, and super-indulgent gluten-free brownie with a soft, and quick-to-make caramel topping

Hacks

The caramel topping on this brownie is not a "proper" caramel, but it's much easier to tackle and still has an amazing flavour. You'll need a thermometer placed in a small saucepan to make it as the temperature you'll heat it to will affect how well the caramel will set. Heating it to 140°C (285°F) means that you need to pour it over the brownie whilst the brownie is still in the tin, (otherwise it will just run down the sides). Using condensed coconut milk is a key hack to helping this set; regular coconut milk won't work as well. Finally, this caramel is incredibly hot and will burn like hell itself if it splashes on your skin, so even if you're hardcore, wear long sleeves and keep stirring as it heats and that will stop (most of) the spitting.

Hazelnut Caramel Buckwheat Brownies (gluten-free)

Make & Bake

Get prepared
» Prepare a 23cm (9") Brownie tin lined with lightly greased baking paper
» If using a chocolate bar rather than drops, chop the Chocolate from Additions section into big chips
» Toast Additions & Decoration Hazelnuts in the oven at 170°C (340°F) for about 8 mins. Roughly chop

Mix the Wet ingredients
» Warm Chocolate Hazelnut Spread & Vanilla Extract in a bowl sitting in another bowl of hot water. Stir & heat to loosen texture

» Add the other Wet ingredients (except the melting Hazelnut Spread & Vanilla Extract) into a mixing bowl or stand mixer bowl
» Using a hand mixer or stand mixer with paddle attachment, mix on speed 3 for 6 minutes, until the sugar is partially dissolved
» Add the softened Hazelnut Spread & Vanilla Extract mixture into the same mixing bowl and mix on speed 3 for 2 minutes

Wet Mix	g	oz
Choc Hazelnut Spread	29	1.0
Vanilla Extract (ethanol)	8	0.3
Olive Oil	207	7.3
Almond Milk	172	6.1
White Caster Sugar	184	6.5
Demerara Sugar	92	3.2

Dry Mix
» Weigh the Baking Powder and keep separate (this is added to the mix at a later stage than the other Dry ingredients)
» Weigh and sieve all the other Dry ingredients into another bowl
» Stir through by hand to ensure the ingredients are evenly distributed. The mixture should be a uniform colour by the end

Dry	g	oz
Baking Powder	8	0.3
Buckwheat Flour	158	5.6
Sea Salt	6	0.2
Cocoa Powder (dutch)	29	1.0
Pea Protein	75	2.6

Mix Wet & Dry together
» Add Dry ingredients (exc Baking Powder) to the Wet in the mixing bowl and start mixing immediately on speed 1 for 45 seconds
» Quickly scrape down and mix again on speed 1 for 45 seconds
» Add Baking Powder and mix on speed 1 for 30 seconds

After mixing
» Add the Chocolate Chips and Hazelnuts and stir through by hand using a spatula for about 30-40 seconds
» Tip mixture out into Brownie tin. Level off with offset palette knife
» Bake immediately for 28 mins or until a toothpick comes out almost clean (totally clean will give you a slightly cakier brownie)
» Leave in the tin, and cool for an hour before making the caramel

Additions	g	oz
Chocolate Chips	47	1.7
Hazelnuts	78	2.8

Bake
180°C (355°F)
for 28 minutes

Decorate

» Weigh out and dice Vegan Butter. Put all ingredients into a saucepan and heat on high temperature for 2-3 minutes
» Continually stir with a whisk as it's heating, (or it'll definitely burn)
» As the temperature reaches 105-110°C (230°F), reduce the heat slightly. You don't want to overshoot the target temperature
» It will start to thicken at around 125°C (260°F), which is normal
» As soon as it hits 140°C (285°F), pour over the brownie (still in the tin), and sprinkle the toasted hazelnuts on top whilst still warm
» Allow to cool for an hour or so, then refrigerate (still in the tin), for at least 3 hours before cutting. Refrigerate again after cutting

Quick Caramel	g	oz
Vegan Baking Butter	126	4.4
Vanilla Extract	5	0.2
Coconut Milk (*condensed)	210	7.4
White Caster Sugar	50	1.8
Muscovado Sugar	30	1.1

Decoration	g	oz
Hazelnuts	47	1.7

Decorated cakes

DECORATED CAKES

Frostings time.

Hacking vegan frostings

This is not an exhaustive list of every type of plant-based frosting, but the main ones that cover a range of textures and richness levels. For each decorated cake, I've matched the cake to the frosting that suits it best.

The Most Natural: seed & nut frostings

These give a satisfying texture with lots of body and suit rustic, homely cakes like Carrot Cake. Nuts or seeds are soaked and after draining, are blended with coconut cream, cocoa butter and icing sugar. The soak time affects the cream's texture and its room stability.

These need a really long blending time to fully smooth out, so they warm up considerably during blending. As a result, they need to be chilled to 10-12°C before using, or they'll lose any shape you've piped with them. Even though they don't smooth out quite as well as the other frostings, this can be improved by melting the cocoa butter before blending.

Cashew Cream - see Carrot Cake recipe
The healthiest frosting in this book, with the lowest levels of both fat and sugar, and a neutral, cream colour.

Sunflower Seed Cream - see Carrot & Sunflower Cupcake recipe
Slightly higher natural fat content gives a slightly richer flavour than the Cashew Cream. Doesn't smooth out quite as well though, and has a slightly grey colour, but it's fantastic as a natural nut-free option.

The Most Chocolatey: ganache frostings

In its simplest form ganache is made by combining 1 part heated cream with 1 part room temperature chocolate; this is known as a '1:1 ratio' ganache.

See Double Chocolate Ganache Layer Cake recipe
The heat from the cream melts the chocolate and then the ingredients are blended until smooth. The ganache is allowed to cool naturally until it reaches approximately 26-28°C (79-82°F), when it's still fluid enough to apply easily, but is starting to thicken. Be aware that once it starts to thicken, it thickens quickly.

Ganache can also be fine-tuned; a higher ratio of chocolate to cream makes a thicker, more room stable ganache, and a lower ratio makes a runnier, more spreadable one.

The Lightest: plant-butter frostings

Higher sugar content makes these sweeter and more room stable than the Seed & Nut Frostings, with a lighter, fluffier texture that really suits cupcakes. Made with plant butter, coconut cream, icing sugar and coconut flour. Shortening has a higher fat content than plant butter so use this for even more room stability and a more neutral base colour.

Fluffy Coconut - see Coconut Kiwi & Lime Cupcake recipe
Pure white colour when made with shortening, with a subtle coconut flavour that pairs beautifully with summery, citrus-flavoured cakes.

Fluffy - see Strawberry Marshmallow Cupcake recipe
A slightly richer, and more neutral flavour than the Fluffy Coconut frosting, this is an amazing all rounder.

The Richest: plant-based buttercream

See Raspberry & Pistachio Traybake recipe
Essentially a plant-based version of traditional Buttercream, with plant butter (or shortening) replacing cow's milk butter. Versatile enough to add cocoa powder for a chocolate flavour, or freeze-dried fruit such as blueberries for a fruity version.

Make sure the icing sugar has no lumps, or you'll have to mix it for so long that the cream will warm up too much to pipe immediately. Instead, whiz the icing sugar for 20 seconds in a food processor first, and the cream will smooth out much more quickly, and remain cool enough to pipe straight away.

The Sweetest: simple icing

Classic Icing - see Simple Iced Lemon Cake recipe
Can be made with just water, but extra delicious when made with an acidic liquid such as lemon juice. Very versatile to colour, by using some fresh fruit rather than lemon juice or water.

The amount of liquid you add to the sugar is key; if you make it runny enough to apply at room temperature, it won't set on your cake. Instead, make it slightly too thick to drizzle on at room temperature and heat it before applying. It will then drizzle easily, and set when it hits a cooled cake.

Super-Nerdy Frostings Guide

Frostings & Icings	Seed & Nut Based		Chocolate Based	Plant Butter Based			Sugar Based
	Cashew	Sunflower	Ganache {1:1 ratio}	Fluffy Coconut	Fluffy	Buttercream	Icing
Mouthfeel	lots of body, creamy	less smooth, & less body than cashew	smooth, lots of body, not light or fluffy	very light, smooth & fluffy		lots of body, fluffy	no body, not fluffy
Best suited for	spreading, (but can be piped)		spreading (when warm), & piping (when a little cooler)	either piping or spreading			drizzling
Best temperature to apply °C (°F)	10-12°C (50-54°F)		26-28°C (79-82°F)	18-20°C (65-68°F)			35°C (95°F)
Room stability	medium to high, (requires chilling first)		high	high		medium; 1-3 hours	medium - high
How easy to make?	most involved, (but not difficult)		easy	easy		very easy	very quick & easy
No. of ingredients (basic)	4	4	2	4	5	2	2
Colour (before colouring)	cream	pale grey	chocolate	white	off-white	cream	white
Fat Content* (approx; depends on fat used for some frostings)	24%	27%	37%	28%	35%	43%	0%
Sugar Content (approx)	26%	26%	16%	48%	48%	48%	84%
Total Sugar & Fat Content (approx)	50%	53%	53%	76%	83%	91%	84%

Fat Content for Plant-Butter Based frostings is highest when using Shortening and lowest when using a Vegan 'Baking Butter'

Carrot & Coconut Cupcakes

(no allergens)

Key Kit
Hand mixer or stand mixer
Oven thermometer
Muffin tin & cupcake cases
Food Processor

Makes
6 cupcakes

Approx Timings
Pre-baking   30 mins
Baking   26 mins
Decoration   15 mins
TOTAL   75 mins
(excluding cooling time)

Storage & Shelf Life
Chilled for 3 days

What to expect
A natural, whole-foods take on a cup cake with no allergens, but no compromises on texture or taste either. Very moist and fluffy, especially for a gluten-free cupcake.

Hacks
Nerd alert. You'll notice that in this recipe, I use half the carrots coarsely grated, and half finely grated.

The finer you grate the carrots the less colourful your crumb will be, as finely grated carrots lose their colour more easily during baking. Coarse carrots on the other hand, can inhibit the binding of the batter, giving a slightly more crumbly texture, which could become a problem here as these cupcakes are gluten-free.

If you don't want the faff of grating at different coarseness levels, grate all the carrot finely rather than coarsely. You won't see those orange flecks as clearly in the crumb, but the flavour will still be lovely.

Carrot & Coconut Cupcakes (no allergens)

Make & Bake

Get prepared
» Chill the Coconut Cream for decoration as early as possible. Wash carrots, trim the tops and tails
» Grate half the carrots coarsely and half finely (see weights in the recipe). Grating carrots creates a small amount of waste, so weigh your carrots after grating, rather than before
» Prepare your muffin tin with cup cake cases so you're ready to portion once mixing has finished
» Pre-heat your oven to 175°C (350°F), ideally with a heavy baking tray inside, (which you'll bake on)

Weigh the Wet ingredients
» Weigh Wet ingredients into a mixing bowl or stand mixer bowl

Wet	g	oz
Plant Milk (allergen free)	75	2.7
Apple Cider Vinegar	14	0.5
White Caster Sugar	130	4.6
Sunflower Oil	34	1.2
Vanilla Extract (ethanol)	5	0.2
Grated Carrots (fine)	81	2.9

Weigh the Dry ingredients
» Sieve all the Dry ingredients from White Rice Flour down to Cinnamon over another bowl
» After sieving, add the Desiccated Coconut and stir through to evenly distribute, until the Dry ingredients are a uniform colour

Dry	g	oz
White Rice Flour	74	2.6
Pea Protein	17	0.6
Arrowroot	17	0.6
Sea Salt	2	0.1
Cinnamon	3	0.1
Desiccated Coconut	49	1.7

Mix Wet & Dry together
» Add the Dry ingredients to the Wet in your mixer bowl
» Using a hand mixer or stand mixer with a paddle attachment, mix on speed 3 for 10 minutes to soften the Desiccated Coconut

Raising Agents
» Add Baking Powder & Bicarbonate of Soda into the mixing bowl
» Using a hand mixer or stand mixer with a paddle attachment, mix on speed 1 for 30 seconds

Raising Agents	g	oz
Baking Powder	8	0.3
Bicarb. of Soda	3	0.1

After mixing
» Using a spatula, stir through the additions by hand
» Using a spoon or a scoop, divide the batter evenly between the cases. If you want to weigh them, each cupcake is 100g (3.5oz)
» Bake immediately, until a toothpick comes out clean

Additions	g	oz
Grated Carrots (coarse)	82	2.9
Currants (or Raisins)	41	1.4

Bake 175°C/ 350°F
for 26 minutes

Carrot & Coconut Cupcakes (no allergens)

Decorate

Get prepared
» Allow cupcakes to cool for at least 1 hour before decorating
» Soak Sunflower Seeds in cold water for 20 minutes
» Use very well chilled Coconut Cream with 85% or 95% coconut content
» Melt Cocoa Butter gently in a bowl over another bowl of hot water. Stir as it's melting

Make the Sunflower Frosting
» Drain the seeds & add to a food processor
» Blend for 2 mins, scraping down every 30 seconds or so
» Add the melted Cocoa Butter, Coconut Cream and Icing Sugar and blend for **15 minutes,** scraping down every 2-3 minutes
» Add a tiny amount of Food Colouring at first, approx 50% yellow and 50% red, and blend for 30 seconds
» Stir, blend again for 30 seconds
» Repeat until you achieve a colour you are happy with
» Put in a piping bag and chill (best temperature to pipe is 10-12°C)
» Decorate with petals, desiccated coconut or whatever you fancy

Frosting	g	oz
Sunflower Seeds	134	4.7
Coconut Cream	138	4.9
Cocoa Butter (melted)	12	0.4
Icing Sugar	100	3.5
Food Colouring	by eye	by eye

Coconut Lime & Kiwi Cupcakes

Key Kit
Hand mixer or stand mixer
Oven thermometer
Muffin tin & cupcake cases
Food Processor

Makes
6 cupcakes

Approx Timings
Pre-baking	20 mins
Baking	24 mins
Decoration	15 mins
TOTAL	60 mins

(excluding cooling time)

Storage & Shelf Life
Chilled for 3 days

What to expect
These zingy & refreshing cupcakes, with their fresh Kiwi core are perfect for Summer. Both the cupcakes & the frosting are super-light & fluffy.

Hacks
If Lime isn't your thing, you can turn these into coconut and kiwi cupcakes by removing the lime juice - just remember to increase the plant milk by the weight of the removed lime juice. Also, as the acidity of the lime juice turbo-charges the effect of the baking powder, if you remove the lime juice, you'll need to compensate by increasing the baking powder to 5g or 6g to achieve the same rise.

Finally, you can use either shortening or plant-based baking butter to make the frosting. If you can't keep these cool, I'd suggest using shortening if you can get hold of it, as its lower water content prevents the frosting melting slightly at room temperature.

Coconut, Kiwi & Lime Cupcakes

Make & Bake

Get prepared
» Chill the Coconut Cream for decoration as early as possible
» Juice and zest the limes (it's around 1 lime for 6 cupcakes)
» Prepare your muffin tin with cup cake cases so you're ready to portion once mixing has finished
» Pre-heat your oven to 165°C (330°F), ideally with a heavy baking tray inside, (which you'll bake on)
» This recipe uses Coconut Plant Milk (usually in a carton), not the coconut milk usually in a can
» Check your Lemon Extract: if it's ethanol based, just use the recipe as it is. If it's oil-based, double the extract to 12g (0.4oz), and reduce the Sunflower Oil to 86g (3.0oz)

Wet Mix
» Weigh Wet ingredients into a mixing bowl or stand mixer bowl
» Use Coconut Plant Milk instead of Soya or Oat Milk for more coconut flavour, (but not the Coconut Milk usually found in a can)
» Using a hand mixer or a stand mixer with a paddle attachment, mix for 3 minutes on Speed 3. The sugar should be partly dissolved by the end of mixing

Wet	g	oz
Plant Milk	78	2.8
Fresh Lime Juice	23	0.8
Sunflower Oil	98	3.4
Lemon Extract (ethanol)	6	0.2
Lime Zest	2	1 tsp
Golden Caster Sugar	168	5.9

Dry Mix
» Weigh and sieve all the Dry ingredients into another bowl
» Stir through by hand to ensure the ingredients are evenly distributed. The mixture should be a uniform colour by the end

Dry	g	oz
White Spelt Flour	168	5.9
Sea Salt	1	pinch
Baking Powder	3	0.1
Pea Protein	20	0.7
Arrowroot	20	0.7

Final Mix
» Add the Dry ingredients to the Wet in the mixing bowl
» Start mixing as soon as possible after adding in the Dry
» Mix on speed 1 for 20 seconds, scrape down
» Mix again on speed 1 for another 20 seconds

After mixing
» Using a spoon or a scoop, divide the batter between cupcakes
» If you want them all exactly the same size use a digital scales and weigh each cup cake at 90g (3.2oz) and bake immediately
» Allow cupcakes to cool fully before moving to the next stage
» Once cool, lightly moisten the surface of the cupcakes with plant milk using a pastry brush, (this will help you core them later)

Bake
165°C (330°F)
for 24 minutes

Coconut, Kiwi & Lime Cupcakes

Decorate

Get prepared

» Use Coconut Cream with 85% or 95% coconut content and make sure it's really cold before starting
» Using Vegan Shortening rather than Vegan Baking Butter will help the cream be room-stable
» This cream is pipe-able straight after making. If working in a hot room, chill for 10 mins before piping
» If you'd like a less sweet cream, halve the icing sugar and make up the weight with coconut flour
» Before starting, if your Icing Sugar is really lumpy, whiz in a food processor to remove the lumps

Make the Coconut Frosting

» Using a paddle attachment, mix the Shortening and the Coconut Cream together for 30 seconds on Speed 3
» Add the Icing Sugar and Coconut Flour and mix on Speed 3 for 1 minute to begin with. Scrape down, and repeat, 1 minute at a time, until the cream is really smooth (this can take 2-4 minutes)
» Chill the cream, but only briefly (10-20 minutes), as it firms quickly

Cream	g	oz
Vegan Shortening	56	2.0
Coconut Cream	34	1.2
Icing Sugar	107	3.8
Coconut Flour	28	1.0

Core and Finish the Cupcakes

» Core the cupcakes about 2/3 deep, using an apple-corer or knife
» Using the same corer, cut chunks of peeled Kiwi the same diameter as the core, and pop the chunks into the cores
» Pipe the Coconut Frosting on top, starting at the centre and working out. (I used a 1M nozzle for the effect as pictured)
» Finish with some sliced Kiwi and Lime Zest

	g	oz
Kiwi to core	73	2.6

	g	oz
Kiwi to decorate	46	1.6
Lime Zest	by eye	by eye

Strawberry & Toasted Marshmallow Cupcakes

Key Kit
Hand mixer or stand mixer
Oven thermometer
Muffin tin & cupcake cases
Food Processor

Makes
6 cupcakes

Approx Timings
Pre-baking	20 mins
Baking	24 mins
Decoration	15 mins
TOTAL	60 mins

(excluding cooling time)

Storage & Shelf Life
Chilled for 3 days

What to expect
Soft, fruity & fluffy cup cakes with a soft-serve-like frosting and a chewy crown of toasted marshmallows.

Hacks
You may be wondering why I've laced the marshmallow around the outside of the cupcake, rather than adding them into the batter. (OK, maybe you aren't.) First-off, marshmallows in the batter have a tendency to "pop" during baking, so when you cut the cupcakes open, rather than seeing lovely chunks of marshmallow in the middle, you just see some gaps, where the marshmallow used to be, before it popped. Not great. Secondly, when you place the marshmallows on top, they gently toast instead of boiling and popping, giving the camp-fire vibe I was going for. Oh yeah, they look prettier as well.

Strawberry & Marshmallow Cupcakes

Make & Bake

Get prepared
» Chill the Coconut Cream for decoration as early as possible
» Prepare your muffin tin with cupcake cases so you're ready to portion once mixing has finished
» Pre-heat your oven to 165°C (330°F), ideally with a heavy baking tray inside, (which you'll bake on)
» If using Freeze-Dried Strawberry pieces rather than powdered, grind the pieces in a domestic coffee grinder until a fine powder. (This isn't essential but does gives a lighter crumb)

Wet Mix

» Mix a tiny amount of Food Colouring with Plant Milk and stir
» Add more food colouring, stirring each time, until the Almond Milk is very bright pink. (Make it pinker than you want the finished cake to be, as adding the other ingredients will dilute the colour)
» Weigh Wet ingredients into a mixing bowl or stand mixer bowl, including the coloured Plant Milk. Using a hand mixer or stand mixer with paddle attachment, mix for 3 minutes on Speed 3

Wet	g	oz
Plant Milk of your choice	78	2.8
Food Colouring	by eye	by eye
Apple Cider Vinegar	14	0.5
Sunflower Oil	89	3.1
Vanilla Extract (ethanol)	6	0.2
Golden Caster Sugar	153	5.4
Freeze-Dried Strawb.	7	0.3

Dry Mix

» Weigh and sieve all the Dry ingredients into another bowl
» Stir through by hand to ensure the ingredients are evenly distributed. The mixture should be a uniform colour by the end

Dry	g	oz
White Spelt Flour	153	5.4
Sea Salt	1	pinch
Baking Powder	4	0.1
Pea Protein	18	0.6
Arrowroot	18	0.6

Final Mix
» Add the Dry ingredients to the Wet in the mixing bowl
» Start mixing as soon as possible after adding in the Dry
» Mix on Speed 1 for 20 seconds, scrape down
» Mix again on Speed 1 for another 20 seconds

After mixing
» Using a spoon or a scoop, divide the batter between the cases
» If using a scales, weigh each cupcake at 85g (3oz).
» Place a ring of Marshmallows on top of the batter around the outside edge, against the cupcake case. Bake immediately
» Allow cupcakes to cool fully before applying the frosting

Additions	g	oz
Marshmallow (vegan)	50	1.8

Bake
165°C (330°F)
for 24 minutes

Strawberry & Marshmallow Cupcakes

Decorate
Get prepared
» Use Coconut Cream with 85% or 95% coconut content and make sure it's really cold before starting
» This cream still works if you swap Shortening for Vegan Baking Butter, (it'll just be less room-stable)
» The cream needs chilling briefly before using. If working in a hot room, chill for 20 mins before piping
» Before starting, if your Icing Sugar is really lumpy, whiz in a food processor first, to remove lumps

Make the Frosting
» Using a paddle attachment, mix the Shortening and the Coconut Cream together for 30 seconds on Speed 1
» Add the Icing Sugar, Cocoa Butter & Coconut Flour. Mix on Speed 3 for 1 minute to begin with. Scrape down, and repeat, 1 minute at a time, until the cream is really smooth (this can take 2-4 minutes)
» Add a tiny amount of Pink Food Colouring. Mix for 10 seconds, on Speed 3 and gradually add more Food Colouring, mixing briefly each time, to achieve the colour you want
» Chill the cream, but only briefly (10-20 minutes), as it firms quickly

Cream	g	oz
Vegan Shortening	58	2.0
Coconut Cream	35	1.2
Icing Sugar	110	3.9
Cocoa Butter	17	0.6
Coconut Flour	11	0.4
Food colouring	by eye	by eye

Finish the Cupcakes
» Slice some Strawberries and place on top of the cupcake. Pipe the Frosting on top. I used a 2A nozzle, piping from outside to inside for this look. Finish with extra Strawberries & Marshmallows

Fresh Strawberry	by eye	by eye
Marshmallows	by eye	by eye

Cream-Core Chocolate Cupcakes

Key Kit
Hand mixer or stand mixer
Oven thermometer
Muffin tin & cupcake cases
Food Processor

Makes
6 cupcakes

Approx Timings
Pre-baking	20 mins
Baking	24 mins
Decoration	15 mins
TOTAL	60 mins

(excluding cooling time)

Storage & Shelf Life
Chilled for 3 days

What to expect
Easy to make, soft & fluffy chocolate cupcakes with an indulgent chocolate butter-cream surprise in the core

Hacks
For these chocolate cupcakes I wanted a light, fluffy texture, so I've steered away from using melted chocolate, because, in general, the more melted chocolate you add to a cake batter, the denser it becomes.

Instead, all the chocolate flavour in these comes from cocoa powder, which means choosing the right cocoa powder is crucial to making these taste deliciously chocolatey. There are two types of cocoa powder; Dutched and Natural. If you can find Dutched, I would definitely recommend it - you'll get a more intense chocolate flavour and a slightly darker, richer crumb.

Cream-Core Chocolate Cupcakes

Make & Bake

Get prepared
» Prepare your muffin tin with cup cake cases so you're ready to portion once mixing has finished
» Pre-heat your oven to 165°C (330°F), ideally with a heavy baking tray inside, (which you'll bake on)
» These are super-quick to make, so it's extra important to pre-heat your oven long before starting

Wet Mix
» Weigh Wet ingredients into a mixing bowl or stand mixer bowl
» Using a hand mixer, or a stand mixer with a paddle attachment, Mix for 3 minutes on Speed 3
» The sugar should be partly dissolved by the end of mixing

Wet	g	oz
Plant Milk of your choice	95	3.3
Apple Cider Vinegar	16	0.6
Sunflower Oil	87	3.1
Vanilla Extract (ethanol)	6	0.2
Golden Caster Sugar	170	6.0

Dry Mix
» Weigh and sieve all the Dry ingredients into another bowl
» Stir through by hand to ensure the ingredients are evenly distributed. The mixture should be a uniform colour by the end

Dry	g	oz
White Spelt Flour	130	4.6
Sea Salt	1	pinch
Baking Powder	6	0.2
Pea Protein	20	0.7
Arrowroot	20	0.7
Cocoa Powder (dutch)	39	1.4

Final Mix
» Add the Dry ingredients to the wet in the mixing bowl
» Start mixing as soon as possible after adding in the Dry
» Mix on Speed 1 for 20 seconds, scrape down
» Mix again on Speed 1 for another 20 seconds

After mixing
» Using a spoon or a scoop, divide the batter between cup cakes
» If using a scales, weigh each cupcake at 90g (3.2oz)
» Bake immediately
» Allow cupcakes to cool fully before applying the frosting

Bake
165°C (330°F)
for 24 minutes

Decorate

Get prepared
» Before starting, if your Icing Sugar is really lumpy, whiz in a food processor first, to remove lumps

Make the Frosting

Cream	g	oz
Vegan Baking Butter	228	8.0
Icing Sugar	228	8.0
Cocoa Powder (dutch)	55	2.0

» Cube the Baking Butter, and using a paddle attachment, beat on Speed 3 for 2 minutes until it's a rough-paste texture
» Add Icing Sugar & Cocoa Powder and mix for 1 minute on speed 1
» Scrape down and mix again on Speed 3 or 4 for 2 mins until fluffy
» This cream is pipe-able straight after making, but if you're working in a hot room, chill for 10 mins before piping

Core and Decorate the Cupcakes

Vegan Chocolate chunks to decorate	by eye	by eye

» Core the cupcakes about 1/2 deep, using an apple-corer or knife
» Pipe the cream by filling all the cores first, then go back to pipe the tops (this helps frost each cupcake with a similar amount)
» For the look in the photos, use a 2D nozzle (sometimes called 852) and start from the outside and work inwards

Raspberry & Pistachio Traybake

(gluten-free)

Key Kit	Approx Timings	
Hand mixer or stand mixer	Pre-baking	30 mins
Oven thermometer	Baking	43 mins
Brownie Tin	Decoration	15 mins
	TOTAL	1hr 28 mins
	(excluding cooling time)	

Makes	Storage & Shelf Life
12 Cake Squares	Chilled for 3 days

What to expect
Moist, tangy, and with a hint of orange, this has a lovely Summery vibe. Really simple to make and decorate

Hacks
Unlike a lot of my other recipes that rely on dried fruit, a shallow cake like this can take fresh fruit very well. You can tweak it and use other berries, (or other nuts) to suit the season or your mood. Firmer berries are best, and slicing them helps to avoid sinking and sogginess. You can also tweak the frosting; for a slightly less rich cake use the cashew cream from my Carrot Cake recipe. Alternatively, if you want to amp up the sweetness, use the Icing from the Iced Lemon Loaf Cake recipe; (you'll need to double up the icing ingredients from that recipe). Or just forget the frosting altogether, and go crazy on the fresh fruit and nuts to decorate - the cake is moist enough in itself to enjoy without a frosting.

Raspberry & Pistachio Traybake (gluten-free)

Make & Bake

Get prepared
» Rinse Raspberries, slice into quarters, drain and dry off
» Shell and chop Pistachios by hand (or using a food processor) until approximately half-sized
» Prepare your brownie tin (ideally one with a removable base), with lightly oiled baking paper
» Pre-heat your oven to 165°C (330°F), ideally with a heavy baking tray inside, (which you'll bake on)

Wet Mix
» Weigh Wet ingredients into a mixing bowl or stand mixer bowl
» Check your Orange Extract: if it's ethanol based, just use the recipe as it is. If it's oil-based, double the extract to 44g (1.6oz) and reduce the Sunflower Oil to 27g (1.0oz)

Wet	g	oz
Almond Milk	219	7.7
Apple Cider Vinegar	28	1.0
Sunflower Oil	71	2.5
Orange Extract (ethanol)	22	0.8
White Caster Sugar	301	10.6

Dry Mix
» Weigh and sieve all the Dry ingredients into another bowl excluding the Ground Almonds (which don't sieve)
» Add the Ground Almonds and stir through by hand to ensure the ingredients are evenly distributed. The mixture should be a uniform colour by the end

Dry	g	oz
Pea Protein	35	1.2
White Rice Flour	149	5.2
Sea Salt	3	0.1
Arrowroot	35	1.2
Ground Almonds	149	5.2

Final Mix
» Add the Dry ingredients to the Wet in the mixing bowl
» Start mixing as soon as possible after adding in the Dry
» Mix on speed 3 for 3 minutes, scrape down
» Mix again on speed 3 for another 3 minutes
» Add raising agents and mix on speed 1 for 30 seconds

Raising Agents	g	oz
Baking Powder	11	0.4
Bicarb. of Soda	1	pinch

After mixing
» Add the Raspberries and Pistachios and stir through to distribute
» Pour batter into the tin and smooth over using a palette knife
» Bake immediately
» Allow to cool in the tin for at least an hour before tipping out

Additions	g	oz
Raspberries (sliced)	150	5.3
Pistachios (chopped)	40	1.4
weight excludes shells		

Bake
165°C (330°F)
for 43 minutes

Decorate

Get prepared
» If your Icing Sugar has lumps, whiz in a food processor to remove them; 1 minute is usually enough

Make the Frosting
» Cube the Baking Butter, and using a paddle attachment, beat on Speed 3 for 1 - 2 minutes until it's a rough-paste texture
» Add the Icing Sugar and the Orange Extract
» Mix gently to start with, on Speed 1 for 1 minute
» Scrape down and mix on Speed 4 for 2 minutes or until light & fluffy, scraping down after every minute or so
» This cream can be used straight away, but if you're working in a hot room, chill for 10 mins before applying

Buttercream	g	oz
Vegan Baking Butter	250	8.8
Icing Sugar	250	8.8
Orange extract (ethanol)	5	0.2

Decorate the Traybake
» Using a spatula or a palette knife, apply the Frosting on the cake
» Finish off with some Fresh Raspberries and Pistachios
» For a clean cut, chill thoroughly before slicing

Decorate	g	oz
Raspberries	60	2.1
Pistachios (chopped)	20	0.7

weight excludes shells

Mocha Marble Loaf Cake

Key Kit
Hand mixer or stand mixer
Oven thermometer
Regular thermometer
Loaf tin, saucepan
Food processor

Makes
1 Loaf Cake (6 portions)

Approx Timings
Pre-baking	20 mins
Baking	75 mins
Decoration	15-20 mins
TOTAL	1hr 50 mins
(excluding cooling time)	

Storage & Shelf Life
Chilled for 3 days

What to expect

Easier than it looks. One batter divided with two flavours and marbled together - a light part with a white chocolate flavour and dark chocolate chunks, and a dark part with coffee flavour from brewed coffee and cocoa powder. A unique texture which is firm at first bite, but melt-in-the-mouth soon after. Topped with a thick coffee and cocoa-flavoured cashew cream made using coconut sugar for some extra caramel notes.

Hacks

There's a little more to this than a regular cake with chocolate and coffee flavours added to it. Replacing a big chunk of the sunflower oil that I would usually use with melted cocoa butter gives both parts of this cake a subtle white chocolate flavour. You'll also notice I've borrowed from the cupcake recipes by replacing some pea protein with arrowroot. This is to help lighten the colour of the light part of the cake. The slight loss of richness this causes is offset by the extra flavour of the cocoa butter. You can increase/decrease the coffee flavour in the cake and cream in two ways: by extending/shortening the brew time of your coffee, or by increasing/decreasing the amount of ground coffee used when brewing.

Mocha Marble Loaf Cake

Make & Bake

Get prepared
» Pre-heat your oven to 160°C (320°F), ideally with a heavy baking tray inside, (which you'll bake on)
» Chop the Chocolate Chips (see Additions section). Prepare loaf tin with a liner and non-stick spray
» Brew filter coffee using 60g of ground coffee with 150g of off-the-boil water. Brew for 1 minute & pour off 60g of coffee needed to soak the Cashews (called '1 min Brewed Coffee' in Cream section).
» Continue to brew remainder for another 2 minutes. Pour off 25g of coffee for the dark batter part ('3 min Brewed Coffee'). Weigh out the other Additions so they are ready to use straight after mixing

Wet Mix
» Heat all Wet ingredients in a saucepan on a medium heat until Cocoa Butter fully melted and mixture reaches 50°C (122°F)
» Pour into a bowl or stand mixer bowl and
» Mix for 2 minute on Speed 3 using a hand mixer, or a stand mixer with a paddle attachment

Wet	g	oz
Cocoa Butter	41	1.4
Vanilla Extract (ethanol)	5	0.2
Maple Syrup	16	0.6
Plant Milk of your choice	122	4.3
Apple Cider Vinegar	24	0.9
Sunflower Oil	61	2.2

Dry Mix
» Weigh and sieve all the Dry ingredients excluding the Caster Sugar into another bowl. Add the Golden Caster Sugar after sieving the other ingredients
» Stir through by hand to ensure the ingredients are evenly distributed. The mixture should be a uniform colour by the end

Dry	g	oz
White Spelt Flour	151	5.3
Sea Salt	2	0.1
Baking Powder	10	0.3
Pea Protein	20	0.7
Arrowroot	20	0.7
Golden Caster Sugar	163	5.7

Final Mix
» Add the Dry ingredients to the Wet in the mixing bowl
» Start mixing immediately on Speed 1 for 15 seconds
» Scrape down and mix again on Speed 1 for another 15 seconds

After mixing
» Split the batter into 2/3 (approx 420g) and 1/3 (approx 210g)
» Add the Plant Milk to the 2/3 of batter and mix on speed 1 for 15 seconds. Stir through the chocolate chips by hand briefly
» Mix the 3 minute Brewed Coffee and Cocoa Powder together and add to the 1/3 of batter. Mix on speed 1 for 15 seconds
» Pour batters into the tin, alternating the light and dark batters
» Using a skewer or knife, zig-zag through the batters to **partly** swirl the light & dark together. Smooth over with a palette knife
» Bake for 75 minutes, or until a toothpick comes out clean

Additions	g	oz
Plant Milk	19	0.7
Dark Chocolate Chips	56	2.0
3 min Brewed Coffee	25	0.9
Cocoa Powder (dutch)	14	0.5

Bake
160°C (320°F)
for 75 minutes

Mocha Marble Loaf Cake

Decorate

Get prepared
» Use Coconut Cream with 85% or 95% coconut content. Soak the Cashews in 60g of 1 min Brewed Coffee for 20 minutes. Melt Cocoa Butter in a bowl over another bowl of hot water

---

Make the Cashew Cream
» **Stage 1:** drain Cashews, and retain 20g of the Brewed Coffee you used to soak the Cashews in, for stage 2. Dispose of the rest
» Add Cashews to the food processor and blend for 30 seconds.
» Scrape down, blend for another 30 seconds

Cream stage 1	g	oz
1 min Brewed Coffee	60	2.1
Cashews	41	1.4

» **Stage 2:** add all other ingredients and blend for 5-6 minutes or until smooth. (It can take 8-10 mins). Scrape down every 2-3 mins
» Refrigerate very thoroughly before decorating, (the ideal temperature for spreading is around 10-12°C)
» Spread cream on top of the cake using a spatula or palette knife
» Finish with chocolate wafers/ vegan choc balls/ white choc drops

Cream stage 2	g	oz
Coconut Cream	55	1.9
Cocoa Butter	14	0.5
Coconut Sugar	37	1.3
1 min Brewed Coffee	20	0.7
Cocoa Powder (dutch)	14	0.5

Cherry Amaretto

Key Kit
Hand mixer or stand mixer
Oven thermometer
2 x round tins 20cm (8")
Food processor

Makes
12 (big) slices

Approx Timings
Pre-baking	30 mins
Baking	44 mins
Decoration	20 mins
TOTAL	1hr 34 mins

(excluding cooling time)

Storage & Shelf Life
Chilled for 3 days

What to expect
Light & fruity enough for an afternoon cake break, but also impressive enough for an after-dinner dessert. Bursting with flavour and colour, this cake has a bright sweet cherry swirl through its light Amaretto crumb, is studded with popping sour cherries and the cocoa butter in the frosting adds an indulgent hint of white chocolate.

Hacks
Key to achieving the 'semi-naked' frosted look is flipping the top layer cake upside down when assembling the cake. When you scrape the frosting tightly on the side of the cake you'll get a flash of cake at the top and bottom, and a band of frosting in the middle. Flipping the top layer also gives a slightly smoother surface on the top of the cake on which to spread your cream.

The recipe has been developed with a mix of fresh and dried cherries in mind. You can substitute the dried cherries with another dried fruit (or leave them out), but as the fresh cherries are pulped and form part of the batter, they can't be left out or substituted with dried cherries, or the cake will be dry. Finally, if you want an alcohol-free version of this cake you can replace the Amaretto with almond extract.

Make & Bake

Get prepared
» Chop the Additions Dried Cherries into small pieces. Blend the fresh/ frozen cherries into a pulp
» If using frozen cherries, allow the pulp to warm up to room temperature (don't refrigerate)
» Chill the Coconut Cream for Decoration. Prepare 2 x 8in round tins & line with lightly greased paper
» Pre-heat your oven to 160°C (320°F), ideally with a heavy baking tray inside, (which you'll bake on)

Wet Mix
» Weigh all Wet ingredients into a bowl or stand mixer bowl
» Using a hand mixer or a stand mixer with paddle attachment, mix for 3 minutes on Speed 3

Wet	g	oz
Almond Milk	191	6.8
Sunflower Oil	191	6.8
Apple Cider Vinegar	42	1.5
Amaretto	53	1.9
Golden Caster Sugar	453	16.0

Dry Mix
» Weigh and sieve all the Dry ingredients, excluding the Ground Almonds, into another bowl. Add the Ground Almonds after sieving the other ingredients
» Stir through by hand to ensure the ingredients are evenly distributed. The mixture should be a uniform colour by the end

Dry	g	oz
White Spelt Flour	340	12.0
Pea Protein	106	3.8
Sea Salt	8	0.3
Baking Powder	11	0.4
Ground Almonds	53	1.9

Final Mix
» Add the Dry ingredients to the Wet in the mixing bowl
» Start mixing as soon as possible after adding in the Dry
» Mix on Speed 1 for 25 seconds, scrape down
» Mix again on Speed 1 for another 25 seconds

Additions
» Divide the batter evenly between two jugs (712g or 25.1oz each)
» Pour around a third of a jug of batter into each tin
» Sprinkle a quarter of the sour cherries on each cake, and drizzle a zig zag with a quarter of the pulped cherries across the top of the batter on each of the tins
» Pour another third of a jug of batter into each tin
» Sprinkle the remainder of the sour cherries, and drizzle a zig zag with the last of the pulped cherries on each of the tins
» Pour the remainder of the batter evenly into both tins
» Stir through the batter just once, to swirl the pulped cherries
» Bake immediately

Additions	g	oz
Dried Sour Cherries	90	3.2
Fresh/Frozen Cherries	120	4.2

Bake
160°C (320°F)
for 44 minutes

Cherry Amaretto Cake

Decorate

Get prepared
» Use Coconut Cream with 85% or 95% coconut content
» Melt the Cocoa Butter in a bowl over another bowl of hot water. Stir as it's melting

Make the Cashew Cream
» Soak Cashews in boiling water for 20 mins, then drain thoroughly
» Add soaked Cashews to a food processor, blitz for 1 minute, scrape down, blitz for 1 minute. Add Cherries, blitz for 1 minute, scrape down, blitz for 1 minute. Add everything else, except the Beetroot Powder, and blitz for 2-3 minutes until really smooth
» Add the Beetroot Powder and blitz briefly for 10-15 seconds
» Divide cream into a larger amount 640g (22.6oz) and smaller amount 160g (5.6oz). The smaller amount is for swirls on top of the cake. For a deeper coloured swirl, add 3g (0.1oz) of Beetroot Powder to the 160g (5.6oz), blend through, transfer to piping bag with nozzle (I used nozzle 1M). Chill all cream for 30-60 minutes
» Once chilled, spread a third of the 640g (22.6oz) cream portion on the bottom layer of cake with a palette knife. Turn the second layer of cake upside down, and place on top of the cream, and spread another third of cream on top of the top layer. Apply the remaining third to the sides of the cake & smooth off the sides with a scraper (this creates a little waste). Using the piping bag, apply swirls to the top of the cake, and finish with fresh cherries

Cream	g	oz
Cashews	212	7.5
Cherry (fresh/ frozen)	72	2.6
Coconut Cream	245	8.7
Cocoa Butter (melted)	14	0.5
Icing Sugar (sifted)	179	6.3
Amaretto	7	0.3
Beetroot Powder (sifted)	7	0.2
Beetroot Powder (sifted; this is optional, for darker swirls)	3	0.1

Carrot Cake with Cashew Cream Frosting

Key Kit
Hand mixer or stand mixer
Oven thermometer
2 x round tins 20cm (8")
Food Processor
(A palette knife is helpful)

Makes
12 good-sized slices

Approx Timings
Pre-baking	30 mins
Baking	43 mins
Decoration	15-20 mins
TOTAL	1hr 30 mins

(excluding cooling time)

Storage & Shelf Life
Chilled for 3 days

What to expect
Two layers of classic Carrot Cake (with a hint of orange), filled and topped with a cashew and coconut cream frosting. Natural deliciousness.

Hacks
When it comes to making the frosting for this cake, you should think of the soak-time for the cashews as an ingredient. The longer you soak the nuts for, the more water they'll absorb, and the wetter, (and therefore less room-stable), your cream will be.

I found that 20 minutes was a sweet spot where the amount of water absorbed by the nuts made the cashews soft enough to be blended into a smooth cream, but firm enough not to be runny at room temperature. Soaking for longer will give a slightly smoother, softer cashew cream, but will require more refrigeration. Your call.

Carrot Cake with Cashew Cream Frosting

Make & Bake

Get prepared
» Chill the Coconut Cream for Decoration as early as possible, ideally overnight
» Wash Carrots, trim the tops and tails. Grate half the Carrots coarsely & half finely (weights in recipe)
» Use 2 x 20cm (8") round tins with lightly greased baking paper & use baking belts for flat layers
» Weigh out the Decoration Nuts and the Additions Nuts separately
» Toast nuts on a baking tray in the oven at 160°C (320°F) for 8 minutes
» Once toasted, chop Additions Nuts coarsely and the Decoration Nuts very finely. If chopping in a food processor, be careful not to over chop or they'll clump together

Weigh the Wet ingredients
» Weigh Wet ingredients into a mixing bowl or stand mixer bowl
» Check your Orange Extract: if it's ethanol based, just use the recipe as it is. If it's oil-based, double the extract to 46g (1.6oz) and reduce the Sunflower Oil to 98g (3.5oz)
» Using a hand mixer or a stand mixer with a paddle attachment, mix on speed 1 for 6 minutes until the sugar partially dissolves

Wet	g	oz
Almond Milk	95	3.3
Apple Cider Vinegar	36	1.3
Orange Extract (ethanol)	23	0.8
Golden Caster Sugar	360	12.7
Sunflower Oil	144	5.1
Carrots (finely grated)	218	7.7

Weigh the Dry ingredients
» Weigh and sieve all the Dry ingredients from White Spelt Flour down to Ground Ginger over another bowl (exclude Ground Almonds as these won't sieve)
» After sieving, add the Ground Almonds and stir through to evenly distribute, until the Dry ingredients are a uniform colour

Dry	g	oz
White Spelt Flour	303	10.7
Pea Protein	90	3.2
Sea Salt	4	0.1
Baking Powder	18	0.6
Bicarb. of Soda	9	0.3
Cinnamon	2	0.1
Ground Ginger	4	0.1
Ground Almonds	76	2.7

Mix Wet & Dry together
» Add the Dry ingredients to the wet in the mixing bowl
» Start mixing immediately and mix on speed 1 for 30 seconds

After mixing
» Using a spatula, stir through the additions by hand
» Divide batter evenly between layers (approx 870g (30.7oz) each)
» Spread evenly with a palette knife
» Bake immediately, until a toothpick comes out clean
» Allow to cool for at least 2 hours before decorating

Additions	g	oz
Carrots (coarsely grated)	214	7.5
Raisins	79	2.8
Walnuts	101	3.6

Bake
160°C (320°F)
for 43 minutes

Decorate

Get prepared
» Use Coconut Cream with 85% or 95% coconut content
» Soak the Cashews in cold water for 20 minutes
» Melt the Cocoa Butter in a bowl over another bowl of hot water. Stir as it's melting

---

Make the Cashew Cream
» Drain Cashews, add to the food processor, blend for 30 seconds
» Scrape down, blend for another 30 seconds
» Add all other ingredients and blend for 5-6 minutes or until smooth. (It can take 8-10 mins). Scrape down every 2-3 mins
» Refrigerate very thoroughly before decorating, (the ideal temperature for spreading is around 10-12°C)
» Using a palette knife, spread half the cream on the bottom layer
» Place second layer on top (don't press down too hard)
» Spread the remaining cream on the top layer
» Sprinkle Walnuts as you like (I used a plate as a stencil)
» Finish with a ribbon of Carrot

Cream	g	oz
Cashews	213	7.5
Coconut Cream	219	7.7
Cocoa Butter	9	0.3
Icing Sugar	159	5.6

Finishing	g	oz
Walnuts (chopped)	25	0.9
Carrot ribbons		

Double Chocolate Ganache Cake

Key Kit
Stand mixer* (or hand mixer)
Oven thermometer
2 x round tins 20cm (8")
Saucepan, Thermometer
Stick blender, Cake comb

Makes
12 (good-sized) slices

Approx Timings
Pre-baking   30 mins
Baking   45 mins
Decoration   30 mins
TOTAL   1hr 45 mins
(excluding cooling time)

Storage & Shelf Life
Chilled for 3 days

What to expect

Two layers of chocolate-chip studded moist chocolate cake, separated and covered with a firm, rich ganache, and finished with some fun, chocolate-covered nuggets of fruit and nuts for extra flavour and texture.

Hacks

Cocoa powder is a tricky thing to bake with; when used at a level that gives a real chocolate flavour (rather than just a chocolate colour), it has a powerful drying effect. This makes for a very crumbly egg-free cake, so this recipe switches from the Pea Protein method to a Chia 'egg' method. With its cocoa powder and chocolate, this can take the loss of flavour of not using Pea Protein but it really needs the moist elasticity provided by the 'egg'. Coconut sugar works really well in this by enriching the chocolate flavour. Substituting with golden caster sugar will make a cake with a more cocoa-like, rather than chocolate-y flavour. The temperature you apply the ganache will make a difference to how smooth your finish will be; there's a fine line between it being too runny and too firm. The sweet spot will vary by the chocolate you use; for mine, it was 26-28°C. If it becomes too cool to apply smoothly, sit the bowl of ganache in another bowl of hot water and stir through to re-melt, and try again.

* This recipe suits a stand mixer more than a hand mixer. It can be mixed using a hand mixer, but you'll need a powerful one to distribute the Chia 'egg' evenly.

Double Chocolate Ganache Layer Cake

Make & Bake

Get prepared
» Pre-heat your oven to 160°C (320°F), ideally with heavy baking trays inside, (which you'll bake on)
» Prepare 2 x 8in round tins & line with lightly greased paper. Use baking belts to make flatter layers
» If using a chocolate bar for the chocolate chips, dice the bar into almond-sized pieces
» If not using pre-ground Chia seeds, grind them for 20 seconds in a domestic coffee grinder until fine
» For the Ganache, use Coconut Cream with 85% or 95% coconut content

Dry Mix
» Weigh and sieve all the Dry ingredients into a bowl (not your main mixing bowl)
» Stir through by hand to ensure the ingredients are evenly distributed. The mixture should be a uniform colour by the end

Dry	g	oz
White Spelt Flour	357	12.6
Cocoa Powder (dutch)	59	2.1
Sea Salt	3	0.1
Ground Coffee	4	0.2
Bicarb. of Soda	3	0.1

Wet Mix
» Add ground Chia Seeds to the Almond Milk in your main mixing bowl or stand mixer bowl. Mix on speed 1 for 20 seconds
» Check your Vanilla Extract: if it's ethanol based, just use the recipe as it is. If it's oil-based, double the extract to 28g (1oz) and reduce the Sunflower Oil to 210g (7.4oz)
» Weigh all other Wet Mix ingredients into the same bowl
» Using a hand mixer, or a stand mixer with paddle, mix on speed 3 for 3 minutes. Scrape down well, and mix on speed 3 for 1 minute
» It's important there are no clumps of Chia seeds at this stage
» Scrape down to check. Mix for another minute if needed

Wet	g	oz
Chia Seeds (ground)	34	1.2
Almond Milk	272	9.6
Sunflower Oil	238	8.4
Apple Cider Vinegar	34	1.2
Vanilla Extract (ethanol)	14	0.5
Coconut Sugar	365	12.9

Final Mix
» Add the Dry ingredients to the Wet in the mixing bowl
» Start mixing as soon as possible after adding in the Dry
» Mix on Speed 1 for 25 seconds, scrape down
» Mix again on Speed 1 for another 25 seconds

Additions
» Add the Chocolate Chips to the batter and stir through by hand
» Divide the batter evenly between each tin, approximately 760g (26.8oz) per tin. Level off with a palette knife. Bake immediately

Additions	g	oz
Chocolate Chips	160	5.7

Bake
160°C (320°F)
for 45 minutes

Decorate

Make the Ganache

» Melt Coconut Cream in a saucepan until it reaches 80°C (176°F)

» Once up to temperature, pour over Chocolate chunks, and stir

» Using a stick blender, blend until very smooth, (takes 2 minutes)

» Scrape bottom of the bowl. Re-blend any lumps until very smooth

» Ganache will be around 37°C (99°F) at this point. Leave to cool until around 30°C (86°F) then, using a hot palette knife, apply a quarter of the ganache on the top layer of cake, and level off

» Allow to set slightly for 5 minutes then flip the other cake upside down and place on top of the first layer. Working quickly, apply another quarter to the top of the top layer, and smooth and level off using a hot palette knife. The ganache will now be slightly cooler, around 28°C (82°F). Apply to sides of the cake and smooth out the sides. If ganache starts to set, melt slightly with a very hot palette knife. Using a cake comb, create grooves on the sides and top whilst the ganache is still fluid

Ganache	g	oz
Chocolate Chips	500	17.7
Coconut Cream	500	17.7
Nuggets	g	oz
Chocolate Chips	115	4.1
Pistachios (chopped)	81	2.9
Sour Cherries (dried)	81	2.9

Make the Nuggets

» Heat the Chocolate in a bowl over another bowl of hot water, add other ingredients, and stir through

» Using a teaspoon, scoop out 12 nuggets onto a plate & before they set, decorate with freeze-dried raspberries, chopped nuts or gold lustre spray. Chill for 10 minutes, before using them to decorate

Desserts

DESSERTS

Desserts for different moods.
Fresh, indulgent, and decadent.

Tiramisu

What to expect

A perfect after-dinner dessert, this super-creamy plant-based version of a Classic Tiramisu combines two layers of soft coffee-flavoured biscuit & smooth cashew cream.

Hacks

This is a great dessert to make a day ahead as both the flavours and textures improve overnight. Some of the ingredients in it have been chosen specifically to give the right colours with just enough contrast between the biscuit and the cream. You can make the biscuit base with a darker sugar such as coconut sugar and get great flavour, but the biscuit will be much darker.

Also, just like my other recipes which make a cream by soaking nuts or seeds, think of the soak time in this recipe as an ingredient. Compared to the cashew cream for the Carrot Cake recipe, the cashews in this recipe are soaked overnight (rather than for 20 minutes), as the nuts need to be very soft to achieve the smoothest, creamiest texture possible. Also, we can use a slightly wetter texture here as the finished product is stored chilled until serving, so there's less risk of the cream warming up and running.

Make & Bake

Get prepared
» **Day before:** soak Cashews overnight in water until the nuts are comfortably covered. You can soak the Cashews in Brewed Coffee or some water with coffee liqueur but this will darken the cream
» Use Coconut Cream with 85% or 95% coconut cream and chill overnight before making the cream
» **On the day:** pre-heat your oven to 175°C (347°F) ideally with a heavy baking tray inside, (which you'll bake on). Prepare your baking tin(s) by lightly greasing. Remove butter from fridge for 15 mins or so

Make the Biscuit Layers
» Combine coffee extract with sugar
» Cream the butter and the sugar/coffee mixture together using a hand mixer or stand mixer and mix on speed 1 for 1 min. Scrape down, mix again on speed 1 for another 1 minute
» By the end there shouldn't be any lumps of butter (if there is, butter was too cold) and it should be quite fluffy

Wet	g	oz
Vegan Baking Butter	247	8.7
Golden Caster Sugar	158	5.6
Coffee Extract (ethanol)	52	1.8

» Add dry ingredients and using a strong spatula, mix these in to the butter mixture. You'll almost have to smear the mixture against the side of the bowl to get it to combine. Stop when there are no more dry ingredients at bottom of bowl
» The top layer needs to be thinner and lighter than the bottom layer to stop the cream being squeezed out during assembly, so divide the mixture 410g (bottom layer) and 340g (top layer)

Dry	g	oz
White Spelt Flour	306	10.8
Baking Powder	9	0.3

» If using one tin and baking base and top separately, spread the top layer first. Chill for 10 minutes, along with mixture for the base
» Mixture is stiff & doesn't spread very easily, but try to spread gently using an offset spatula, dipped frequently in very hot water. Try to make the layer as flat as possible. It will look like there's not enough mix to cover the tin. (There is).

» Bake. Allow to cool for 30 mins, then remove the top layer from tin and repeat the spreading and baking process for the larger, bottom layer. (Remember to grease the tin again)
» If using two baking tins and baking top and bottom layer together just spread the mixture into both tins and bake together

Bake
175°C (347°F)
for 12 minutes

» After baking, leave the bottom layer in its tin and loosen around the edges using a palette knife. Remove top layer from its tin and store flat. You can store it on top of the bottom layer in the same tin (it might need trimming). Chill both layers until assembly starts

Tiramisu

Cream & Assemble

Get prepared
» Brew coffee in a cafetiere with 30g of ground coffee and 120g of off-the-boil hot water (yes, you can use instant). Brew for 3 minutes and pour off the separate weights for the Cream and the Drizzle

Make the Cashew Cream & Drizzle
» **Cream:** drain Cashews, and blitz in a food processor for 1 minute
» Scrape down, add the Icing Sugar, blitz for another 1 minute
» Scrape down, add Brewed Coffee, blitz for another 1 minute
» Scrape down, add Coconut Cream, blitz for another 1 minute
» Scrape down, blitz for another 1-2 minutes or until very smooth
» Divide equally into 2 containers and chill for at least 1 hour
» **Drizzle:** thoroughly stir the Brewed Coffee and Coffee Extract

Cream	g	oz
Cashews	331	11.7
Icing Sugar	225	8.0
Brewed Coffee	8	0.3
Coconut Cream	400	14.1

Drizzle	g	oz
Coffee Extract (ethanol)	2	0.1
Brewed Coffee	49	1.7

Assembly
» Remove both biscuit layers from fridge, put top layer aside, leave bottom layer in the tin. Brush half the Drizzle on the bottom layer
» Add one half of the cream on top of the Drizzle, spread level
» Dust with cocoa all over. Place the top layer of biscuit on top of the cocoa and brush the other half of Drizzle on top of this layer
» Add the other half of cream and spread level. Dust with cocoa, (using a cooling rack as a stencil to achieve the look in the photos)
» Chill for 1 hour before serving. Best made the day before serving

Dusting
Cocoa Powder (dutch)　by eye　by eye

Mango Cheesecake

(raw, gluten-free)

Key Kit

Ramekins
  (check yours are freezer friendly if you're planning to freeze the cheesecakes)
Food Processor

Makes
6 little cheesecakes

Approx Timings

Base	10-15 mins
Cream	10-15 mins
Assembly	10 mins
TOTAL	30 - 40 mins

(excluding cooling time)

Storage & Shelf Life
Chilled for 3 days

What to expect
A citrus-y refreshing 'cheesecake' made with cashews rather than store-bought cream cheese, which gives this more body than my Peppermint Cheesecake recipe, but it's more nutritious and just as creamy.

Hacks
The recipe for the coconut base uses dried dates; you can substitute for fresh dates, but these are stickier, so you'll need to reduce the maple syrup a little to compensate.

You can make the base without maple syrup altogether if you prefer, and you'll get a softer, less chewy texture. To do this you'll need to soak dried dates for an hour in warm water first; this will replace the moisture that the maple syrup brings to the standard recipe. For a slightly chewier textured base with an even bigger Summery flavour, replace the dates with dried mango pieces.

Mango Cheesecake (raw, gluten-free)

Make & Assemble

Get prepared
» **The day before:** soak the Cashews overnight in Fresh Lemon Juice and Water (see Cream stage)
» **On the day:** gently melt Coconut Oil in a bowl over another bowl of hot water. Stir as melting

Make the Base
» Chop Almonds in food processor until chunky breadcrumb sized (you need them coarser than shop bought ground almonds)
» Add Dates and continue to chop until Dates are small pieces
» Add all other ingredients and blend until mixture is evenly distributed, and has a slightly sticky breadcrumb texture
» You'll have achieved the right texture when the mixture comes together when it's pressed. Portion 30g (1.1oz) into each ramekin
» Press down firmly and evenly. Refrigerate

Biscuit	g	oz
Whole Almonds	74	2.6
Dried Dates (chopped)	66	2.3
Maple Syrup	21	0.8
Desiccated Coconut	25	0.9
Cinnamon	3	0.1
Sea Salt	1	pinch

Make the Cream
» Soak Cashews overnight with Lemon Juice and Water (approx 400g of water) to comfortably cover nuts. You'll need less than 1 Lemon; this is optional but adds to the citrus, fresh flavour
» Drain Cashews and blitz in a food processor for 1 minute
» Scrape down. Add Maple Syrup, Coconut Oil and Lemon Extract
» Blitz for 1 minute. Scrape down and add Mango Pulp, & blitz for 2-3 minutes until really smooth, scraping down as necessary
» Divide the mixture equally between 2 containers; you'll use one to make a lighter cream, and one to make a darker cream
» To make the darker cream, add the Turmeric to one of the containers and stir through thoroughly.

Cream	g	oz
Cashews	110	3.9
Fresh Lemon Juice	30	1.1
Water to soak	by eye	by eye
Maple Syrup	74	2.6
Coconut Oil (melted)	74	2.6
Lemon Extract (ethanol)	10	0.3
Mango Pulp (canned)	200	7.1
Dried Turmeric (ground)	3	pinch

Assembly & Finishing
» Remove bases from fridge and portion 40g (1.4oz) of the lighter cream on to each base, lightly pressing down to ensure cream doesn't have any air pockets. Smooth the top until it's level
» Add a swirl of Mango Pulp on top of the cream (approx 2g per cake) with a teaspoon. Add 40g (1.4oz) of darker cream on top of the mango swirl, (taking care not to press it into the layers below)
» Smooth top using back of a spoon/ spatula/ offset palette knife
» Freeze for at least 2 hours, then refrigerate until serving
» You can freeze overnight (or longer); allow at least 1-2 hrs to defrost in the fridge, before serving in the ramekins
» Finish with Desiccated Coconut and Pomegranate Seeds

Assembly	g	oz
Mango Pulp (canned)	12	0.4

Finishing		
Desiccated Coconut	by eye	by eye
Pomegranate Seeds	by eye	by eye

Chocolate Raspberry Avo Mousse

(raw option, gluten-free)

Key Kit
Oven thermometer
Oven-proof ramekins
Food processor

Makes
6 Mousses

Approx Timings
Base	10-15 mins
Baking	0-16 mins
Mousse	15 mins
TOTAL	25 - 46 mins

(excluding cooling time)

Storage & Shelf Life
Chilled for 3 days

What to expect
Smooth, creamy chocolate mousse made from avocado, raspberries & maple syrup, with a contrasting textured base made from ground almonds & coconut sugar. Quick to make, no refined sugar, and tons of natural indulgence

Hacks
The base on this can be raw or baked. It's delicious either way, but the baked version takes on a deliciously chewy texture which contrasts even better with the smooth creamy mousse. Also, I've used coconut sugar in the base to add a lovely caramel-type flavour, but if you fancy a slightly plainer base, (or just want to use a more affordable sugar), this recipe is flexible enough for you to substitute for any (granulated) sugar. Finally, the mousse is **really** easy to make; the only thing to be aware of is the ripeness of the avocados; ripe ones blend more easily, and have a creamier texture than under-ripe ones.

Chocolate Raspberry Avo Mousse (gluten-free)

Make, (optional Bake) & Assemble

Get prepared
» Melt the Chocolate for the Mousse in a bowl over another bowl of hot water. Stir occasionally
» Dice cold Vegan Baking Butter into small cubes and keep chilled until needed in the recipe
» Baking the bases is optional. If you are baking, pre-heat your oven to 160°C (320°F)
» Lightly grease your ramekins with non-stick spray

Make the Base
» Add all ingredients into a bowl and rub together until it forms a breadcrumb-like texture and the butter is evenly distributed
» Portion equally into ramekins, each one is around 30g (1oz)
» Press mixture down firmly and flatten. Chill
» If baking, bake once your oven is up to temperature and after baking, allow to cool for 30 minutes, and store in the fridge

Base	g	oz
Ground Almonds	91	3.2
Cocoa Powder (dutch)	9	0.3
Vegan Baking Butter	40	1.4
Coconut Sugar	40	1.4

Bake (optional)
160°C (320°F) for 16 minutes

Make the Mousse
» Blitz raspberries in a food processor until puréed. To achieve a completely smooth mousse, remove the pips out of the purée by forcing it through a sieve. To achieve the weight of de-pipped Raspberries in the recipe (88g) you'll need more Raspberries to start with (120g), as de-pipping creates waste in the sieve
» Peel and remove stones from the Avocados to achieve the correct weight of flesh. You'll need about 2 medium Avocados
» Add Avocado to the food processor and blitz until smooth
» Add Raspberries and all the other ingredients to the Avocado in the food processor and blitz again. Scrape down the sides & bottom after 1 minute, and as necessary. It takes around 2 minutes but continue until you achieve a smooth texture

Mousse	g	oz
Raspberries (de-pipped)	88	3.1
Avocado (flesh only)	246	8.7
Maple Syrup	120	4.2
Chocolate (melted)	70	2.5
Cocoa Powder (dutch)	22	0.8
Sea Salt	1	pinch

Assembly
» When bases are cool to the touch, portion 90g (3.2oz) of mousse onto each base using a spoon or a piping bag, and smooth with the back of a spoon. Chill for at least an hour before serving

Finishing
» Finish with Fresh Raspberries, melted chocolate drizzle or chocolate decorations. To make chocolate 'Zig-Zags' decoration as in the photographs, melt some Chocolate and drizzle onto some baking paper in any shape you want. Chill for at least 30 minutes, then peel off the paper and use to decorate

Finishing	g	oz
Chocolate	40	1.4
Raspberries	48	1.7

Peppermint Cheesecake

Key Kit
Hand mixer or stand mixer
Spring-form or removable
    base 8" (20cm) round tin
Food Processor (optional)

Approx Timings
Base	10 mins
Cream	10-15 mins
Decoration	10 mins
TOTAL	30-35 mins

(excluding cooling time)

Makes
12 portions

Storage & Shelf Life
Chilled for 3 days

What to expect
Refreshing and indulgent; think Mint Choc Chip ice-cream, but as a luxurious cheesecake. One of the quickest recipes to make in this book, as it uses pre-bought ingredients, rather than making each component totally from scratch.

Hacks
You can boost the mint flavour of this in two ways: by using mint flavoured biscuits (I've used mint-flavoured Oreos, but any biscuits work), and by using mint flavoured chocolate for your choc chips. Cream cheese next - whilst specialist whole-food stores now stock several different types, I've used the most readily available type in the UK which is coconut oil based (the brand was Violife). This has a mild flavour and gives good stability to the texture. Finally, to achieve a lovely minty green colour, I've used a little food colouring, but you can use matcha powder if you prefer. You'll need at least 5g (0.2oz) of matcha to achieve even a subtle green colour, but bear in mind that matcha has quite a strong, slightly bitter taste that can dilute the delicious peppermint flavour, so add it gradually, and taste as you go, chef-style.

Peppermint Cheesecake

Make & Assemble

Get prepared

» Line bottom of your baking tin with lightly greased baking paper. You'll need a 'spring-form' tin or one with a removable base to remove the cheesecake when finished
» Chop chocolate into chips if using a bar

Make the Base

» Melt the Baking Butter in a bowl inside another bowl of hot water
» Blitz Biscuits in a food processor until they are small crumbs
» If you don't have a food processor, you can put the biscuits in a plastic bag, and smash them with a rolling pin
» Transfer crumbed biscuits to a bowl and add the melted Butter
» Mix to combine thoroughly, then press into your prepared tin and ensure the mixture is tightly packed, and flat. Refrigerate

Base	g	oz
Vegan Baking Butter	107	3.8
Crushed Oreos (including the cream)	350	12.4

Make the Cream

» Sieve the Icing Sugar to remove lumps
» Add all Cream ingredients, except the Food Colouring and the Chocolate Chips, to a bowl. Using a hand mixer or stand mixer with paddle, whip on speed 3 until evenly blended & creamy
» Scrape down occasionally. Whipping takes around 2 minutes
» Add the Food Colouring carefully in **very** small amounts at a time
» Gently & thoroughly stir through the Colouring each time by hand before adding more. Repeat until you achieve a colour you like
» Gently stir through the Chocolate Chips

Cream	g	oz
Cream Cheese (vegan)	479	16.9
Greek-Style/Thick Yoghurt (vegan)	300	10.6
Peppermint Extract	17	0.6
Fresh Lemon Juice	25	0.9
Icing Sugar	175	6.2
Food Colouring	by eye	by eye
Choc Chips (70% cocoa)	113	4.0

Assembly

» Remove base from fridge; spoon cream on top of the base
» Using a spoon or offset pallet knife, smooth and level the top
» Refrigerate for at least 4 hours, ideally overnight

Decoration

» Melt the Chocolate in a bowl inside another bowl of hot water
» Once melted, pour on to a large piece of baking paper
» Spread out with a pallet knife & make a rough rectangle, A5 size
» Roll the paper up into a tube - the tightness of the tube will affect the shape of the 'shards'. Refrigerate the roll for at least an hour
» Unroll the paper gently and the shards should crack themselves away from the paper. Gently pile them on top of your cheesecake & top with fresh mint to boost the mint flavour even more

Decoration	g	oz
Choc Chips (70% cocoa)	102	3.6

Cookies & biscuits

COOKIES & BISCUITS

The quickest-to-make things in the book.

Different cookies need different methods

The best approach depends on what type of cookie you're trying to make.

Biscuity Cookies

These have a soft-crunch texture that's closest to a traditional biscuit, with a slightly crumbly texture, that's neither chewy nor gooey.

Replacing the butter is best achieved by using plant-based 'baking butter'. Tests with sunflower and coconut oil gave significantly poorer results, even when tested at different levels, and used in different ways.

Getting the best out of 'baking butter' involves the traditional 'crumbing' method. Firstly, sugar and 'baking butter' are combined until the sugar is absorbed. Then flour is added and 'crumbed' (dry mixed) with the butter and sugar. This coats the flour in fat, preventing gluten from developing which would give an unwanted chewy texture. Finally, a tiny amount of liquid is added to bring the dough together, with minimal mixing.

Fantastic results are possible without the need for an egg replacer. The functional properties of eggs that are so essential to giving cakes structure and lift are not essential to make delicious biscuity cookies.

Chewy Cookies

Achieving a more dense, chewy and moist cookie requires adding extra binding in the form of 'Chia Eggs'. This involves mixing chia seeds in water or plant milk, and leaving the mixture to thicken before adding it to the cookie dough. Whole chia seeds can be used, but they give a crunchy mouth-feel. Grinding them beforehand avoids this problem, and allows less to be used for the same binding effect; (chia seeds dilute sweetness, so the fewer you use, the more delicious your cookie).

The subtlety here is the time the Chia Egg is allowed to stand before adding it to the mix. If the stand time is too long, Chia Eggs become very thick, and don't mix well with the rest of the dough due to the slow, short mixing time. Allowing only a short stand time solves this problem, so as soon as the Chia Egg is made, the rest of the process should continue uninterrupted.

Also, the Chia Egg should be added to the sugar and butter mixture *before* adding the dry ingredients. Not only will this ensure the 'egg' doesn't fully set, allowing it to mix with the dry ingredients, but it will also come into direct contact with the flour and develop a little gluten, helping to achieve the chewy texture.

Other ingredients also help make a lovely moist chewy cookie; darker sugars like muscovado, and dried fruits like dates, apricots and figs.

Gooey Cookies (Levain-style)

These huge (170g or 6oz) cookies are influenced by Levain Bakery in New York and have a free-form dome shape, with a slightly under-baked, gooey crumb and a crunchy shell.

A series of tests using aquafaba, chia seeds, pea protein and just plant milk showed that these cookies also don't need a direct egg replacer. What's more critical to these cookies is their shaping and cooling before baking.

The other two cookie types rely on a traditional shaping technique, where the shape of the cookies before baking is generally retained during baking. Achieving a Gooey cookie relies on a different technique, where the dough is shaped into a ball and allowed to flow during baking.

The other two types of cookies can be baked immediately after shaping, or chilled and baked later; either way, the results are similar. For Gooey cookies, it's essential to chill them for at least 90 minutes before baking.

The combination of shaping these into balls, chilling them very thoroughly, and baking them slightly hotter allows the interior to be only just baked by the time the outside, in contrast, is deliciously crunchy.

Gluten-free variants of these cookies need a different approach. The lack of gluten in the flour means the dough isn't extensible enough to flow in the oven. 'Flax Eggs' made with sunflower oil instead of water allow more flow than regular Chia Eggs, preventing the dough from cracking.

However, Flax Eggs only allow about 50% of the flow needed, so a helping hand is required from a tweak to the shaping. Forming gluten-free gooey cookies slightly flatter than gluten-based ones means they bake almost the same shape, and while they're not quite as gooey as the gluten-based ones, they're still super-moist and delicious.

Cranberry & Cardamom Biscuity Cookies

Key Kit
Made by hand or with a stand mixer
Oven thermometer

Approx Timings

Pre-baking	15 mins
Baking	13 mins
Chilling dough	optional
TOTAL	28 mins+

(excluding cooling time)

Makes
6 large cookies

Storage & Shelf Life
Room temp. for 3 days

What to expect
A wholesome cookie made with rolled oats, tangy cranberries and fragrant cardamom. Lower in sugar than the other cookies in this book, and only uses coconut sugar & demerara. This is at the lower end of the indulgence scale, making it a great everyday cookie.

Hacks
Like most biscuits, these need minimal handling to achieve a lovely crumbliness and avoid a tough texture. When shaping, don't over-work them trying to create perfectly round shapes - they look their best as rustic, organic-looking cookies.

Instead, concentrate a little on making them the same thickness right up to the edges. If the cookies taper down to a thin edge rather than having a vertical "shoulder", the edges will bake much quicker than the centre of the cookie and risk burning.

Cranberry & Cardamom Biscuity Cookies

Make

Get prepared
» Ensure Vegan Baking Butter is very cold. Dice into small chunks; keep chilled until you need to use

Dry Mix
» Weigh the Dry ingredients and dry mix thoroughly to ensure all ingredients are evenly distributed. No need to sieve these

Dry	g	oz
White Spelt Flour	131	4.6
Baking Powder	11	0.4
Sea Salt	2	pinch
Cardamom (ground)	11	0.4

Wet Mix 1
» Mix Plant Milk & Orange Extract together using a hand whisk and set aside. *You'll need an ethanol based extract for these cookies, not an oil-based one

Wet Mix 1	g	oz
Plant Milk of your choice	13	0.5
Orange Extract (ethanol)	11	0.4

Wet Mix 2
» Add Vegan Baking Butter and both sugars into a mixing bowl or stand mixer bowl
» Combine by hand by squeezing the Sugar into the Butter, or use a stand mixer with a paddle, and mix on Speed 1 for 30 seconds

Wet Mix 2	g	oz
Vegan Baking Butter	110	3.9
Coconut Sugar	42	1.5
Demerara Sugar	42	1.5

Combine Wet Mix 2 and Dry Mix
» Add the Dry ingredients to the mixing bowl and rub together with your hands until you achieve a breadcrumb texture or using a stand mixer with a paddle, mix on Speed 1 for 30 seconds

Additions & Final Mix
» Add the Additions, and mix through by hand or mix on a stand mixer with paddle on Speed 1 for around 15 seconds
» Add the Wet Mix 1 and combine by hand or using a stand mixer with a paddle, mix on Speed 1 for 15 seconds, until there's no flour at the bottom of the bowl. Stop as soon as combined.

Additions	g	oz
Cranberries	102	3.6
Jumbo Rolled Oats	36	1.3

After mixing
» Weigh into individual cookies; each one is 80g (2.8oz)
» Gently bring the dough together into a ball, and flatten into a rustic round. You can flatten them between 2 sheets of baking paper if they are a little sticky

Cranberry & Cardamom Biscuity Cookies

Bake

» Chill your cookies whilst your oven is heating
» Preheat a baking tray inside the oven whilst the oven is heating
» Make sure your oven is fully pre-heated before baking
» Bake cookies on top of a sheet of baking paper on the hot tray

Storing

» Wrap well and store unbaked for 3 days in the fridge
» Or store in the freezer for up to a month, in a sealed freezer bag. If freezing, defrost fully in the fridge before baking. This takes at least 2-3 hours, so defrosting overnight is easiest
» Once defrosted, bake from chilled, as you do for fresh ones

Bake
190°C (375°F) for 13 minutes

or Store
chilled for 3 days or frozen for up to a month, in a sealed freezer bag. If freezing, defrost fully in the fridge before baking. This takes at least 2-3 hours, so defrosting overnight is easiest.

Once defrosted, bake from chilled, as you do for fresh ones

Date, Pecan & Chia Chewy Cookies

Key Kit
Made by hand or with a stand mixer
Oven thermometer

Makes
6 large cookies

Approx Timings

Pre-baking	20 mins
Baking	22 mins
Chilling dough	optional
TOTAL	42 mins +

(excluding cooling time)

Storage & Shelf Life
Room temp. for 3 days

What to expect
Dense, moist and very chewy cookies, with a deep, sweet flavour from muscovado, dried dates and toasted pecans.

Hacks
There are three types of sugar (yes three) in these cookies, to achieve a bit more depth of flavour. If these cookies were a piece of music you'd hear loads of deep bass (from the muscovado), plenty of mid-range (from the demerara) and just enough sweet treble (from the golden caster sugar) all coming together in perfect harmony.

Time is an ingredient in making these. As soon as the chia seeds have been mixed with the plant milk, the process should continue uninterrupted to prevent the 'eggs' from over-setting. You have been warned.

Date, Pecan & Chia Chewy Cookies

Make

Get prepared
» Weigh out the Pecans and toast in the oven for 8 minutes at 160°C (320°F). Once cool, break in half
» Rinse (but don't soak) your Dried Dates, and allow to drain very thoroughly
» There is lots of scraping down between stages in this recipe, to keep the mix time short
» Ensure Vegan Butter is very cold. Dice into small chunks and keep chilled until you need to use it

Dry Mix
» Weigh the Dry ingredients and dry mix thoroughly to ensure all ingredients are evenly distributed

Dry	g	oz
White Spelt Flour	154	5.4
Baking Powder	3	0.1
Bicarb. of Soda	1	pinch
Sea Salt	2	pinch
Cinnamon	4	0.1

Wet Mix 1
» Weigh Wet ingredients into a mixing bowl or stand mixer bowl
» Don't mix these quite yet (trust me)

Wet Mix 1	g	oz
Vegan Baking Butter	112	4.0
Muscovado Sugar	60	2.1
Demerara Sugar	45	1.6
Golden Caster Sugar	30	1.1

Wet Mix 2 - "Chia Egg"
» If you aren't using pre-ground Chia Seeds, grind whole Chia Seeds in a domestic coffee grinder for 15 seconds until very fine
» Add the Almond Milk & Vanilla Extract to the ground Chia Seeds to make a "Chia Egg", stir through and set aside
» *Go to the next stage immediately or the "Chia Egg" will over-set, and not properly incorporate at the next stage

Wet Mix 2	g	oz
Chia Seeds (ground)	18	0.6
Almond Milk	28	1.0
Vanilla Extract (ethanol)	14	0.5

Combine Wet Mix 1 and Wet Mix 2
» Mix the Sugar and Butter you weighed out in Wet Mix Stage 1
» Combine by hand by squeezing the Sugar into the Butter, or use a stand mixer with a paddle, and mix on Speed 1 for 15 seconds
» Add the Wet Mix 2 "Chia Egg"
» Mix by hand or with a stand mixer on Speed 1 for 15 seconds
» Scrape down, and mix again either by hand or on Speed 1 for 10 seconds. The Chia Egg should have broken up slightly and started to distribute itself in the Butter and Sugar mix mixture

Date, Pecan & Chia Chewy Cookies

Mix Wet & Dry together
» Add the Dry ingredients to the Wet in the mixing bowl
» Mix by hand for approximately 15 seconds, or use a stand mixer with paddle on Speed 1. Scrape down before the next stage

Additions
» Add the Additions, and mix again by hand for around 15 seconds or use a stand mixer on Speed 1 Mix until just incorporated

Additions	g	oz
Pecans	69	2.4
Dried, Diced Dates	138	4.9

After mixing
» Weigh into individual cookies; each one is 110g (3.9oz)
» Gently bring the dough together, and flatten such that the cookies are roughly the same thickness from centre to edge
» Decorate the top with a Pecan or two

Bake
160°C (320°F) for 22 minutes

or Store
chilled for 3 days or frozen for up to a month, in a sealed freezer bag. If freezing, defrost fully in the fridge before baking. This takes at least 2-3 hours, so defrosting overnight is easiest. Once defrosted, bake from chilled, as you do for fresh ones

Bake
» Preheat your baking tray in the oven whilst the oven is heating
» Make sure your oven is fully pre-heated before baking
» Bake cookies on top of a sheet of baking paper on the hot tray
» Using two sheets of baking paper prevents the bottoms burning

Chocolate & Walnut Levain-Style Gooey Cookies

Key Kit	Approx Timings	
Made by hand or with a stand mixer	Pre-baking	20 mins
Oven thermometer	Baking	20 mins
	Chilling dough	60 mins+
	TOTAL	100 mins

Makes	Storage & Shelf Life
6 VERY large Cookies	Room temp. for 3 days

What to expect
An absolute beast of a cookie (170g or 6oz) these are my plant-based version on Levain Bakery's famous gooey cookies. Crunchy on the outside, just-baked on the inside, this recipe takes cookies to another level.

Hacks
These cookies are shaped and baked as dough balls, rather than being patted flat into a cookie shape, and this is key to delaying the baking of the centre which helps give that gooey inside. So you might be wondering, if they flow in the oven so much that they come out lower than when they went in, why does the recipe need raising agents? The cookies I tested without raising agents hardly flowed at all, were much smaller and tighter, and were very soggy rather than deliciously gooey inside. It turns out, the raising agents don't really raise the cookies, they just open up the cookie dough and slacken it enough to allow it to flow. How interesting.

Chocolate & Walnut Gooey Cookies

Make

Get prepared
» Toast the Additions Walnuts in the oven for 7 minutes at 180°C (355°F) and after they've cooled, break or chop them approximately in half. Chop Additions Chocolate into almond-sized chunks
» Ensure Vegan Butter is very cold. Dice into small chunks and keep chilled until you need to use it

Wet Mix
» Add Vegan Baking Butter into a mixing bowl and add the Sugars
» Combine by hand by squeezing the Sugar into the Butter, or use a stand mixer with a paddle, and mix on Speed 1 for 30 seconds
» Scrape down before the next stage

Wet	g	oz
Vegan Baking Butter	184	6.5
Golden Caster Sugar	110	3.9
White Caster Sugar	110	3.9

Dry Mix
» Weigh all the Dry ingredients and mix thoroughly by hand to evenly distribute the ingredients (no need to sieve them)
» Add the Dry ingredients to the mixing bowl and mix for 30 seconds by hand or using a mixer with a paddle on Speed 1
» Scrape down again before the next stage

Dry	g	oz
White Spelt Flour	343	12.1
Baking Powder	5	0.2
Bicarb. of Soda	1	1/4 tsp
Sea Salt	5	0.2

Additions
» Add the Chocolate Chips and toasted Walnuts and mix for 15 seconds by hand or using a mixer with a paddle on Speed 1
» Scrape down again before the next stage

Additions	g	oz
Vegan Chocolate	200	7.0
Walnuts	53	1.9

Final Mix
» Add the Almond Milk and Vanilla Extract and mix for 15 seconds by hand or using a mixer with a paddle on Speed 1

Wet (cont)	g	oz
Almond Milk	31	1.1
Vanilla Extract (ethanol)	10	0.4

After mixing
» Weigh into individual cookies; each one is 170g (6oz)
» Gently bring the dough together into a ball shape. Don't over-mould these into a tight, super-smooth round ball or they won't flow as well during baking. You're aiming for a rustic look here
» Chill for at least 90 minutes or 60 minutes in the freezer. This is key to the gooey inside, as it slows down the bake of the middle of the cookie so it remains slightly under-baked

Chocolate & Walnut Gooey Cookies

Bake

» Preheat a baking tray in the oven whilst the oven is heating
» Make sure your oven is fully pre-heated before baking
» If the oven is not hot enough, you won't achieve that combination of a crunchy outside with that lovely gooey inside
» Don't pat the cookie balls flat before baking, bake them as balls (see right) and they'll flow in the oven
» Bake on a sheet of baking paper, on the pre-heated baking tray

Pre-Oven Shaping Gooey cookies

Bake
190°C (375°F) for 20 minutes

or Store
chilled for 3 days or frozen for up to a month, in a sealed freezer bag. If freezing, defrost fully in the fridge before baking. This takes at least 2-3 hours, so defrosting overnight is easiest.

Once defrosted, bake from chilled, as you do for fresh ones

Raspberry & White Chocolate Gooey Cookies

(gluten-free)

Key Kit
Made by hand or with a stand mixer
Oven thermometer

Approx Timings
Pre-baking	20 mins
Baking	17 mins
Chilling dough	60 mins+
TOTAL	97 mins

Makes
6 VERY large cookies

Storage & Shelf Life
Room temp. for 3 days

What to expect
Huge (170g or 6oz) rustic cookies, with big raspberry flavour, studded with white chocolate. Almost as gooey as the gluten-based Gooey Cookies, with a deliciously super-moist crumb.

Hacks
These need to be shaped mid-way between the other cookies in this book. Whereas the Biscuity and Chewy cookies need shaping flat, and the Chocolate & Walnut Gooey cookies need shaping into balls, these need to be partly flattened balls. This delays the baking of the inside (giving a very moist crumb) whilst still allowing some flow during baking.

Pre - oven shaping

Raspberry & White Choc. Gooey Cookies (gluten-free)

Make

Get prepared
» If using **powdered** Freeze Dried Raspberries, follow the recipe as is. If using **pieces** of Freeze Dried Raspberries, grind in a domestic coffee grinder for 15 seconds until a fine powder
» If using **ready-milled** Flax seeds, follow the recipe as is. If using **whole** Flax seeds, grind the seeds for 15 seconds and set aside
» Ensure Vegan Butter is very cold. Dice into small chunks and keep chilled until the recipe needs it
» Weigh out Raspberries and dice White Chocolate into big chunks (roughly half a Brazil nut size)

Dry Mix
» Weigh all the Dry ingredients and stir thoroughly by hand to evenly distribute the ingredients (no need to sieve them)
» Set aside Dry Mix
» * From here on, you have to continue uninterrupted *

Dry Mix	g	oz
White Rice Flour	167	5.9
Ground Almonds	167	5.9
Baking Powder	25	0.9
Sea Salt	5	0.2

Wet Mix 1
» Mix Almond Milk & a tiny amount of Pink Food Colouring & whisk
» Gradually add more colouring until you get a very deep pink

» Add the ground Gold Flax and Sunflower Oil to the coloured Almond Milk mixture, and hand whisk. Set aside, but go straight to the next stage with no delay, or the Flax mixture, (the "Flax Eggs"), will over-set & not incorporate properly at the next stage

Wet Mix 1	g	oz
Food Colouring	by eye	by eye
Almond Milk	43	1.5
Sunflower Oil	62	2.2
Gold Flax (ground)	27	1.0

Wet Mix 2
» Add Freeze-Dried Raspberries to the Sugar and stir thoroughly
» Place the Vegan Baking Butter into a mixing bowl or stand mixer bowl, and add the Sugar/ Raspberry mixture
» Combine by hand by squeezing the Sugar into the Butter, or use a stand mixer with a paddle, and mix on Speed 1 for 30 seconds
» Scrape down before the next stage

Wet Mix 2	g	oz
Freeze Dried Raspberries (ground)	5	0.2
Vegan Baking Butter	124	4.4
White Caster Sugar	210	7.4

Mix Dry and Wet Mix 2 together
» Add the Dry ingredients to the mixing bowl and mix for 30 seconds by hand or using a mixer with a paddle on Speed 1
» (Keep Wet Mix 1 aside for the moment)
» Scrape down again before the next stage